Escape to Yountville

Sally James and Villagio Inn & Spa
Photography by Alan Benson

1⊖
TEN SPEED PRESS
Berkeley | Toronto

Dedication

To Timothy and Donna Egan for their kindness, generous spirit, enduring support, and commitment to the community of Yountville.

A Kirsty Melville Book

Ten Speed Press
P.O. Box 7123
Berkeley, California, 94707

Distributed in Australia by Simon and Schuster Australia, in Canada by Ten Speed Press Canada, in New Zealand by Southern Publishers Group, in South Africa by Real Books, and in the United Kingdom and Europe by Airlift Book Company.

Library of Congress Cataloging-in-Publication Data

James, Sally, 1959-
  Escape to Yountville : recipes for health and relaxation from the Napa Valley / Sally James and Villagio Inn & Spa ; photography by Alan Benson.
    p. cm.
Includes index.
  ISBN 1-58008-492-3
  1. Cookery, American. 2. Cookery—California—Yountville. I. Villagio Inn & Spa. II. Title.
  TX715 .J267 2003
  641.5973—dc21

                                    2003005010

First printing, 2003
Printed in China
1 2 3 4 5 6 7 8 9 10 - 06 05 04 03

Acknowledgments

It has been a great honor for me to write *Escape to Yountville* and an experience I have enjoyed immensely. In the process of collecting and writing, I had the privilege of meeting and working with so many wonderful people. I am hugely indebted to those who have assisted in the creation of this book, without whom I could not have hoped to write it. Those people are all as much a part of this book as I, and I thank them.

The management and owners of Villagio Inn & Spa, particularly David Shipman and Tim, Donna, and Kerry Egan, who gave me the opportunity to write this book for them. For your belief in the vision, support, and excitement, thank you so much.

All the fine chefs of Yountville who contributed to this book with such enthusiasm and shared an essence of their lives with me.

Yountville chefs cool off in Villagio's fountain. From left to right: Stefan Richter, Villagio Inn & Spa and Cucina à la Carte; Kinyon Gordon (standing), Kinyon Café & Catering; Sebastien Rouxel, Bouchon Bakery; Jeff Cerciello, Bouchon; Jude Wilmoth, Napa Valley Grille; Cindy Pawlcyn, Mustards; Bob Hurley (standing), Hurley's, Peter Hall, Piatti; Eric Torralba, Domaine Chandon; Sally James, author; Thomas Keller, The French Laundry; Mari Jennings, Gordon's; Julio Garcia, Pacific Blues; Alfonso Navarro, Compadres; Philippe Jeanty, Bistro Jeanty.

For your willingness to participate, your cooperation and patience (and getting in the fountain) I thank you all.

Kirsty Melville, publisher at Ten Speed Press, my sincere thanks for believing in the project, and to my patient and enthusiastic editor, Annie Nelson, and wonderful designer, Nancy Austin.

Phil Huettenhain of the Vintage 1870 Wine Cellar for selecting wines to match most of the recipes, for his intuitive advice and sharing his wealth of knowledge and patiently putting up with so many tastings with me. And of course, the always charming David Bridges who chose the wines for Domaine Chandon's dishes.

Steve Zanetell of Yountville Health & Fitness, for his advice on exercise and fitness, and Terri Beckham for spa tips. And to interior designer Charles DeLisle of Your Space and architect Bruce Pao of IPA Design, for their advice on color choices.

Photographer Alan Benson, for always delivering brilliant visions. And to Holly Swedberg for assistance, and Peter Diggs, Jerry Alexander, and Holly Swedberg, for additional photography.

Michael Ward and friends, for allowing me to photograph their beautiful horses at Panchas.

Joe Mills, my tireless and enthusiastic assistant who prepared many of the dishes for photography.

The staff at Villagio Inn & Spa who volunteered tips along the way, including "JJ" Springfield, Leda Tar, and Paul Boudinot; Mary Crowe for her great support, recipe, and tableware; and Kathryn Kenney for cheese and wine pairing information. And to all the other friendly and professional staff who were always there to offer a helping hand and interest.

"Adventures Aloft," for taking the photographer and editor on a breathtaking photo shoot balloon ride.

My husband, who shared the creative vision for this book and was my backbone, support, tireless editor, coordinator of loose ends, loving companion, and reason for being here and writing this book, Stephen Andrews, I love you. And to my patient and encouraging stepdaughters, Samantha and Emily, who for so long have put up with me saying, "Not right now, I'm on a deadline."

And finally, to the people who are and have made the magical town and culinary mecca of Yountville what it is, a huge thanks, simply for doing it so well and giving me a great picture to paint.

Escape to Yountville

*Recipes for Health and Relaxation
from the Napa Valley*

Chefs' Acknowledgments

Behind every great chef is a great team. Many of the chefs of Yountville would like to express their personal thanks to individuals who have helped in the process of compiling their recipes for this book.

Thomas Keller of The French Laundry would like to acknowledge his pastry Chef Sebastien Rouxel, as well as Eric Ziebold and Kristine Keefer for their assistance. Philippe Jeanty of Bistro Jeanty thanks Doug Weldon. Cindy Pawlcyn of Mustards thanks her dedicated pastry chef, Wendy Schuvring. Eric Torralba of Domaine Chandon thanks his team, particularly sous chef Chris Manning. Kinyon Gordon thanks Margaret May for introducing him to the business of food. Julio Garcia thanks Jeff Steen for bringing him to Pacific Blues. Alfonso Navarro is very grateful of the support of Rick Enos. Ryan Jackson conveys his gratitude to his manager, Curt Jones. Mari Jennings is very appreciative of Julie Donoho's support and, of course, thanks Sally Gordon. Jude Wilmoth of Napa Valley Grille thanks Derek De La Paz. Bob Hurley expresses his gratefulness to Jerry Lampe and his wife, Cynthia, for their unwavering support through thick and thin. Finally, Stefan Richter at Cucina à la Carte and Villagio Inn & Spa would like to convey sincere gratitude to his entire team.

Prop Acknowledgments

Thanks to the following stores at Vintage 1870 in Yountville for providing tableware for the food photographs: Cravings, Cucina à la Carte, The Barrel Cellar, Regent Jewelry & Gifts, and A Little Romance.

Also to Bison Australia, available at Vintage 1870 and selected stores, and Napa sculptor Victoria Pinter for some of the exquisite ceramics in the book. And to H&H Design and Carpets Unlimited in Napa for the beautiful tiles.

Contents

From the Bounty of Napa Valley

Everyday Spa: Luxurious Recipes for Life

Introduction

I first discovered Yountville in 1999, during a trip I made to the United States to attend a culinary conference in Rhode Island. On my flight out from Australia, I'd picked up a magazine and learned that the Napa Valley town of Yountville was the home of Thomas Keller and his acclaimed restaurant, The French Laundry. I'd previously encountered Thomas in Versailles, France, to receive awards for our cookbooks, but never knew The French Laundry was located in this little culinary mecca.

When the conference was over, I had a little time to spare before returning to Australia. San Francisco had always been one of my favorite cities to visit, but I'd never made it to the renowned wine country just over an hour away. This seemed the ideal opportunity to visit this region I'd so longed to see and write a story on some of the chefs of the valley for my magazine.

I was put in touch with the media whiz of Napa, Jan Austerman, who organized my accommodations in the relaxed, pampering elegance of the Villagio Inn & Spa, right in the center of Yountville. Instantly I sensed a magical charm surrounding the town and an energy that was exciting yet restful, serious yet carefree. I was enthralled by the number and diversity of the restaurants, all seemingly brimming full of energy, enthusiasm, and camaraderie. The

ambience of the town was magnetic, and I found myself not wanting to travel any further into the valley to write the feature.

As it turned out, I was looked after a little too well by Villagio's director of Media and Communications, Stephen Andrews, and the town of Yountville wasn't all I fell in love with. Soon I had the good fortune of becoming Mrs. Stephen Andrews and living amid all this beauty.

Perhaps one of the best ways for me to paint you a picture of this town of Yountville I've come to love is to take you on a visual and aromatic tour of my morning run. It's midfall, and I head out past the gurgling fountains and landscaped grounds of Villagio. I turn onto Washington Street, where early risers are enjoying coffee on the deck of Pacific Blues. Wafting across the street come the aromas of baking focaccia escaping from Hurley's intermingled with that classic French boulangerie bouquet from Bouchon Bakery. (Am I in Italy? France?)

Further on, groups of balloonists, still in wondrous awe, are devouring a Mexican breakfast and champagne on the grassy slopes of Compadres. Joggers and walkers, most with dogs, are in abundance and all greeting one another as I head up toward the enchanted corner of The French Laundry. I breathe in the clean, fresh-pressed aromas surrounding the historic house, scented with a background of stocks being prepared for the day's delicacies.

Turning down Yount Mill Road to head toward the vineyards, I'm greeted by the crowds enjoying the fresh cakes, breads, and ful-filling breakfasts at Gordon's Café & Wine Bar. Next door, the only

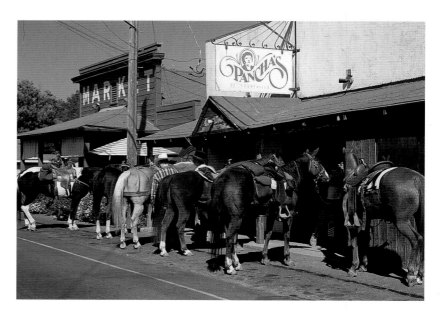

signs of life at Pancha's—the local watering hole—are the well-worn hitching posts and wells of water waiting for horses to bring in their riders for a beer or two later on.

Into the sweeping floor of vineyards, that heady, intoxicating fragrance of grapes being harvested fills the air. The sun is reflecting off the turning fall leaves on the vines like a golden carpet. The road turns and follows along a meandering creek shrouded by a dense canopy of trees. Here I encounter the more serious cyclists and runners partaking in their morning constitutional.

Coming toward me, I recognize the groups of workers heading off to tend the vines, and I return their smiles and waves.

Suddenly the avenue of trees gives way to bright sunshine and another vineyard vista, this time amid hills dotted with wineries, from rustic Tuscan style to New England classic.

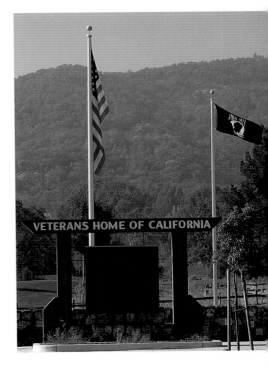

As I arrive back on the highway for the return leg, Mustards Grill is already in full swing serving its classic comfort food. I run past the Yountville Cemetery, where George Yount, the town's pioneer founder, is buried, and head home past fields of corn, sunflowers, and pumpkins. I take a shortcut through some back streets lined with everything from quaint cottages to rambling homes surrounded by spacious verandas. Near the end of my run, I see early-morning golfers waiting for mists to lift off the greens, as flocks of ducks fly in for their day of paddling on the course's lake. Perched behind the hillside, like a sentinel standing watch over the town, sits the famous, grand Veterans Home, a historic institution where many of Yountville's colorful and active community members reside.

I am amazed how a town of this diversity and charm can maintain such a wonderful sense of quaintness—definitely a credit to the locals, restaurateurs, hotels, and business owners. It is a huge honor for me to be able to write this book to give you a glimpse into this small magical town and bring you an essence of its food and lifestyle.

Like the town itself, *Escape to Yountville* is balanced indulgence for the mind, body, and soul. In the pages that follow, you will find recipes from Yountville's chefs and a get a peek into their lives, passions, and health rituals. More than a cookbook, *Escape to Yountville* also provides you with ideas and tips for bringing a taste of this town into your own home and life—whether spa ideas from Villagio, exercise tips from the Yountville gym, or more recipes for internal and external pleasure and relaxation.

I hope this book will inspire you to enhance your days with the Yountville lifestyle—and excite you to come and experience an escape to Yountville yourself.

—Sally James and Villagio Inn & Spa

Yountville—the Heart of the Napa Valley—Past to Present

In 1836, pioneer settler George Calvert Yount first set eyes upon the Napa Valley and declared, "In such a place I should love to clear the land and make my home. In such a place I should love to live and die."

Yountville is a town rich in history. After all, it was here in 1838 that Yountville's founder, George C. Yount, planted the first grapevine cutting to the fertile soil of Napa Valley, giving birth to the region's wine industry; in 1870 that the historic 23-acre Groezinger Winery Estate (on which the Villagio Inn & Spa now sits) was constructed; and in 1884 that the magnificent 500-acre Veterans Home of California at Yountville was founded by veterans from the Mexican-American and Civil Wars.

Through the years, Yountville has carefully retained its rural wine-country charm and residential character, blending the history and culture of the past with the culinary and viticultural triumphs of the present day.

Annual Celebrations

Trumpeting its sense of occasion, Yountville celebrates with signature events for every season. From the rich heritage of local culture to the pageantry of the holidays, the seasons in Yountville come to life with festivals, celebrations, and special events.

From the day after Thanksgiving to New Year's Day, the **Yountville Festival of Lights** celebrates the magic of the yuletide with the entire town festooned in sparkling white lights.

February through March is mustard season in the Napa Valley— fields of wild mustard paint the vineyards and rolling hills yellow. The **Napa Valley Mustard Festival** showcases the season with a series of world-class culinary events. As the birthplace of the festival, Yountville presents its finest in food, wine, and hospitality during **A Taste of Yountville,** a daylong homage to epicurean adventure where festival-goers can sample everything definitively "Yountville."

From May through October, the **Yountville Farmer's Market** offers the bounty of the season with sumptuous fresh produce from

around the region. During that period, June brings the annual **Father's Day Invitational Auto Show** to the Vintage 1870 specialty shops complex when more than 85 autos spanning 100 years of production roll into town.

October heralds community pride with the **Yountville Days Parade & Festival** in celebration of hometown spirit. And **Yountville's Epicurean Affair** presents an unparalleled five-month series of programs pairing the town's famed chefs and winemakers for tours, tastings, demonstrations, and dinners.

All in all, no small feat for a little hamlet measuring just a mile in length.

About Suggested Wine Pairings

With each suggested wine pairing, I encourage readers to think beyond standard selections. Wine should make the food more enjoyable and vice versa. It should be as much about the occasion as the dish being served. So I have offered a classic choice and an adventurous or "rule breaker" choice for each recipe. After all, escape and relaxation is all about adventure.

Have fun and bon appétit!

All wine pairings by Phil Huetten-hain, Vintage 1870 Wine Cellar, unless otherwise noted.

Escape to Yountville

Starters

Parma Prosciutto Wraps with Balsamic Dipping Oil | 4

Salmon and Smoked Trout Rillette | 7

Asparagus and Smoked Salmon Filo Spirals | 8

Red Wine and Pepper Crackers with Pear–White Wine Pâté | 9

Nori-Crusted Ahi Tuna Sashimi with Hijiki Seaweed Salad | 10

Grape and Almond Gazpacho | 15

Mari's Chilled Cherry Tomato Gazpacho | 16

Pumpkin and Apple Soup | 18

White Bean Minestrone with Garlic and Parmesan Bruschetta | 20

Cream of Artichoke Soup with Lemon Pesto | 21

Parma Prosciutto Wraps with Balsamic Dipping Oil, page 4

SERVES 6

Balsamic Dipping Oil

1 tablespoon balsamic vinegar
3 tablespoons extra virgin olive oil
Pinch of chile flakes
1/2 teaspoon chopped fresh garlic
1/2 teaspoon chopped fresh parsley

Prosciutto Wraps

6 thin slices Parma prosciutto
1/2 pound (about 24) baby Blue
    Lake beans, or French green
    beans
1 handful mixed garden greens
1 tablespoon extra virgin olive oil
Juice of 1 lemon
2 tablespoons toasted pine nuts
    (see note)
2 tablespoons freshly grated
    Parmesan cheese
Freshly ground black pepper

Parma Prosciutto Wraps with Balsamic Dipping Oil

There couldn't be a simpler, more appetizing starter that captures the essence of rural Italian cooking than these wraps. This creation of Peter Hall's introduces the thread that continues through his menus—taking fresh seasonal and local produce, tossing in a few classic Italian elements and techniques, and presenting the dish in a way that makes you want to reach out and start before the plate's even landed. When you make these yourself, you can cut them in half to serve as hors d'oeuvres, or make a stack of three for a salad course.

To prepare the dipping oil, combine the vinegar, olive oil, chile flakes, garlic, and parsley in a shallow saucer; set aside.

To prepare the prosciutto wraps, lay the prosciutto slices out on a board. Place the beans and the greens in a medium bowl, and drizzle with the olive oil and lemon juice. Add the pine nuts and Parmesan, toss well, and season to taste with pepper. Gather four of the beans along with a small handful of the greens and pine nut mixture, and place across one end of each prosciutto slice. Beginning at the filled end of the slice, roll up to form a cigar shape. Continue with the remaining ingredients. Serve immediately, with the dipping oil on the side.

Note: To toast the pine nuts, place them in a skillet over medium-high heat. Toss them continuously in the skillet until they begin to turn a light golden color. Transfer the pine nuts to a plate and spread them out in a single layer to cool.

CLASSIC: MEDIUM-DRY SHERRY
ADVENTUROUS: MODERATELY AGED SPARKLING BLANC DE BLANCS

PETER HALL, PIATTI

Peter Hall is a chef with energy, drive, and passion. He is a man who has grown to realize that good food and eating well can make a huge difference in how you feel—and his restaurant's food has evolved to reflect this philosophy.

When you dine at Piatti, you'll find Peter intensely working over the grill in his open kitchen, or finishing off a dish while jesting with his staff. Look up again and he's at a table greeting friends and offering suggestions. Peter has brought not only a sense of playful creativity and sophistication to Piatti's menu, but also a tradition of going back to basics, making some of his own prosciutto, cheeses, olive oil, and cured fish, and sometimes he's even seen foraging in local hills for mushrooms. At Piatti you can expect fresh, sensitively simple fare.

Yountville has added to his life in many ways. He enjoys his walk to work and having easy access to San Francisco, a city whose energy he loves. He also believes Yountville has become a spotlight to the world and a culinary mecca, yet seemingly without outgrowing the small-town feel. Peter finds that he is also able to be personally healthier as a chef in Yountville.

This energized chef's rituals include destressing by starting every day with stretching and working out in the local gym. His underlying ethic, however, is threefold—to treat his staff with respect and friendship, to have passion for what he does, and above all, not to take life too seriously.

Salmon and Smoked Trout Rillette

JEFF CERCIELLO
BOUCHON

Leave it to the chic French restaurant Bouchon to prepare such a wonderful version of rillette—the perfect starter to set the scene and pace of a meal. This recipe makes enough for about fifteen people. If you only need half that amount, make the full recipe, divide it in half, and seal the jar with clarified butter.

To cook the salmon, trim and discard any dark flesh or bloodline from the salmon. Place the salmon in a shallow nonreactive baking dish and sprinkle it on both sides with the kosher salt, white pepper, and Pernod. Cover and refrigerate for 1 hour, turning the salmon halfway through the marinating process.

Fill a shallow steamer, large enough to hold the salmon, with 2 to 3 inches of water, and bring to a boil over high heat. Place the salmon in the steamer and cover with a lid. Decrease the heat to medium-low and slowly steam until no more than medium-rare, about 8 minutes (if you see steam escaping out the sides from under the lid, lower the heat to maintain a gentle steam. To check for doneness, slice into the center of the salmon after steaming for 8 minutes; the fish should be moist and pink in the center. Remove the salmon from the steamer and let cool.

In a sauté pan over medium heat, melt 2 tablespoons of the butter. Add the shallots and cook gently to sweat, about 2 minutes. Add the 1/2 teaspoon salt and continue to cook until the shallots have softened but not browned, 3 to 4 minutes longer. Remove the pan from the heat, and let the mixture cool.

Place the remaining butter in a mixing bowl and beat with a wooden spoon until smooth (similar in consistency to mayonnaise). Stir in the crème fraîche; set aside.

Place the cooled salmon in a large mixing bowl and break it into large chunks (it will continue to be stirred, so don't break up the pieces too finely). Add the smoked trout, shallot mixture, lemon juice, olive oil, and egg yolks. Season to taste with salt and white pepper (since this is to be served cold, be sure that the seasonings are assertive). Fold in the butter and crème fraîche mixture. Place the mixture in small glass jars or a crock, leaving a space of at least 1/2 inch on top. Refrigerate for 1 hour to chill before serving. Serve cold, spread on the toasted baguette slices.

CLASSIC: SPARKLING BLANC DE NOIRS OR A RICH CHARDONNAY
ADVENTUROUS: PINOT NOIR (ANDERSON VALLEY)

SERVES 15

1 pound center-cut salmon fillet (approximately 1 to 1 1/2 inches thick), skin and bones removed

1 tablespoon kosher salt

1/2 teaspoon freshly ground white pepper, plus more as needed

2 tablespoons Pernod

1/2 cup unsalted butter, at room temperature

1/2 cup minced shallots

1/2 teaspoon salt, plus more as needed

1 tablespoon crème fraîche

1/2 pound cold-smoked, whole trout fillets, skinned, boned, and finely diced, at room temperature

2 tablespoons freshly squeezed lemon juice

1 tablespoon extra virgin olive oil

2 egg yolks, lightly beaten (see note)

Clarified butter, if needed (see note)

Toasted baguette slices

Notes:

* If you have doubts about using raw eggs, you can substitute a pasteurized egg product instead.

* If you are not using the rillette within in a day or two, pour melted clarified butter over the top of the rillette to a depth of 1/4 inch to seal, cover, and keep refrigerated for up to 2 weeks. To serve, lift the clarified butter off the top of the rillette, and discard. Once the butter seal is lifted, use the rillette within 2 days.

Asparagus and Smoked Salmon Filo Spirals

MAKES 12 SPIRALS

3 tablespoons finely grated
Parmesan cheese

1 tablespoon freshly grated
lemon zest

2 teaspoons freshly ground black
pepper

6 sheets filo pastry, thawed if frozen

Lemon-infused olive oil or extra
virgin olive oil, for brushing
pastry

12 to 14 ounces smoked salmon
cut into 12 thin slices

12 thick spears fresh asparagus,
ends trimmed

Paprika, for sprinkling

Reduced Balsamic Drizzle

1/2 cup balsamic vinegar

1 teaspoon brown sugar

It seems that as soon as a wisp of spring is in the air, the markets and restaurant menus of Yountville and the Napa Valley are abuzz with plump, tender, local asparagus. One of my favorite ways to bring out the flavor of this versatile vegetable is to roast it. For a treat, I like to wrap asparagus spears in smoked salmon before winding them with strips of delicate filo. Finished with a drizzle of reduced balsamic vinegar, these elegant spirals make great pre-dinner nibbles.

Preheat the oven to 425°F. Line a baking sheet with parchment paper or lightly brush it with oil.

Combine the Parmesan, lemon zest, and pepper in a small bowl; set aside.

On a dry, flat work surface, lay out 1 sheet of filo. Fold the filo in half lengthwise, lightly brush the top with oil, and sprinkle the oiled surface with about 2 teaspoons of the Parmesan mixture. Cut it in half lengthwise to form 2 strips. Wrap 1 slice of salmon around 1 spear of asparagus. Working from the base of the asparagus to the tip, carefully wrap 1 of the filo strips (seasoned side toward the asparagus) around the asparagus in a spiral. Repeat with the remaining ingredients. Place the spirals on the prepared baking sheet, brush the tops lightly with olive oil, and sprinkle with paprika. Bake for 10 to 12 minutes, until golden brown. Serve immediately, drizzled with reduced balsamic vinegar.

To make the balsamic drizzle, place the vinegar and brown sugar in a small saucepan. Bring the contents to a boil, then decrease the heat and simmer for 5 to 10 minutes, or until thickened to a syrup.

CLASSIC: VIOGNIER
ADVENTUROUS: GAMAY BEAUJOLAIS

Red Wine and Pepper Crackers
with Pear-White Wine Pâté

This is my favorite cracker and dip combination to serve in front of a roaring fire with some sliced autumn pear, olives, and a glass of rich red wine. The flavors of pears and red wine are a sublime match—a true Napa Valley indulgence!

To prepare the crackers, stir together the flour and wheat germ into a large bowl, and then make a well in the center. In a medium bowl, whisk together the wine, olive oil, and buttermilk, and pour into the well. Using a knife, mix quickly and gently until the dough just comes together. Turn the dough out onto a lightly floured board and knead to form a smooth dough. Cover with plastic wrap and refrigerate for 30 minutes.

Preheat the oven to 375°F.

Cut a piece of parchment paper to fit one large or two small baking sheets. Roll the dough out on the parchment paper to a thickness of about 1/4 to 1/8 inch. Brush the dough with egg white and sprinkle with pepper. Using a sharp knife, trim the edges of the dough and score it into 2-inch squares, cutting most, but not all, of the way through the dough. Lift the parchment paper directly onto the baking sheet. Place in the oven and bake for 15 to 20 minutes, until golden brown and crisp. Transfer the sheets of crackers to a wire rack to cool. Remove from the parchment after cooling, then break into individual crackers. The crackers will keep in a sealed container at room temperature for up to 1 month.

To prepare the pâté, place the pears and white wine in a small, non-reactive saucepan over high heat and bring to a boil. Decrease the heat to low and simmer until the pears are tender and have absorbed most of the wine, 20 to 30 minutes. Remove the pan from the heat and allow the pears to cool. Place the pears in a food processor or blender, add the lemon zest and Parmesan, and process until well blended. With the motor running, slowly add the olive oil and process just until the mixture starts to thicken. Season to taste with pepper. Transfer the pâté to a glass or ceramic bowl, cover with plastic wrap, and refrigerate for at least 1 hour to allow the pâté to thicken and the flavors to develop. Serve cold or at room temperature with the crackers. The pâté will keep, tightly covered and refrigerated, for 2 to 3 days.

CLASSIC: DRY RIESLING OR BLANC DE NOIRS
ADVENTUROUS: GAMAY BEAUJOLAIS

MAKES ABOUT 4 DOZEN CRACKERS

1 cup flour
1/2 cup wheat germ or oat bran
1/4 cup Cabernet, Merlot, or other rich, bold red wine
1/4 cup extra virgin olive oil
1/4 cup buttermilk
1 egg white, lightly beaten, for brushing
Freshly ground black pepper

Pear-White Wine Pâté

MAKES ABOUT 1 CUP

2 ripe seasonal pears, peeled and diced
1 cup dry white wine, such as a fruity Chardonnay or Sauvignon Blanc
1 teaspoon freshly grated lemon zest
2 tablespoons freshly grated Parmesan cheese
1 to 2 teaspoons extra virgin olive oil
Freshly ground black pepper

C

SERVES 4

Ahi Sashimi

12 ounces sashimi-grade ahi tuna

4 ounces nori furikake (a seasoned
    seaweed-sesame blend found
    in Asian markets and most
    specialty markets)

Blend of half sesame and half
    canola oil for searing

Vinaigrette

2 tablespoons rice wine vinegar

2 tablespoons soy sauce

6 tablespoons sesame oil

Salad

1 carrot, peeled and finely
    julienned

3 ounces mung bean sprouts

2 ounces hijiki seaweed (soaked
    in water and drained)

2 ounces wakame seaweed (soaked
    in water and drained)

2 tablespoons toasted sesame
    seeds (see note)

Soy sauce, as accompaniment

Wasabi paste, as accompaniment

Nori-Crusted Ahi Tuna Sashimi with Hijiki Seaweed Salad

This dish, in one form or another, has become a signature menu item at Brix, where Chef Ryan Jackson has taken it from a towering spiral to this artistic spread. When purchasing the tuna for this recipe, be sure to ask for it to be sashimi grade—and very fresh. You'll find the seaweed and Asian ingredients in the Asian section of most supermarkets or specialty stores.

To prepare the sashimi, cut the ahi into 4 equal pieces. Pour the nori furikake onto a large plate, and roll each piece of ahi in the mixture to coat well on all sides. Heat a large, nonstick sauté pan over high heat until hot. Add enough of the oil blend to just coat the bottom of the pan and heat the oil until very hot. Add the ahi and quickly sear, just 2 seconds per side.

To prepare the salad, whisk together the vinaigrette ingredients in a small bowl. In a medium bowl, combine the carrot, bean sprouts, seaweeds, and sesame seeds, add the dressing, and toss well; set aside.

To serve, slice the ahi into 1/4-inch-thick slices and arrange on 4 individual plates. Divide the salad among the plates. Serve immediately, with soy sauce and wasabi paste for dipping.

Note: To toast the sesame seeds, place them in a skillet over medium-high heat. Toss them continuously in the skillet until they begin to turn a light golden color. Transfer the seeds to a plate and spread them out in a single layer to cool.

CLASSIC: SAUVIGNON BLANC
ADVENTUROUS: PINOT NOIR

C

RYAN JACKSON, BRIX

Coming from a family of fruit growers, Ryan Jackson brought to Brix a healthy respect for the land's produce as well as classic traditions of farm life, such as family meals to enjoy the fruits of their labor.

His career in the Napa Valley began at Domaine Chandon, where he learned to appreciate the essence of the French cooking techniques, but with a lighter hand, under the influence of Robert Curry. He then joined the team at Brix and was able to help shape the cuisine of the restaurant as it evolved.

Ryan loves Brix's panoramic garden, which provides over eight different ingredients for the menu every season, allowing chefs the opportunity to create home-grown dishes and take the story of the dish to Brix diners. Additionally, the friendliness of this small community, the camaraderie of the neighboring chefs, and the opportunity to make friends with the farmers, makes Yountville a desirable location for Ryan to call home.

To the casual yet elegant ambience of Brix, Ryan delivers a quality of food that is designed to wow the diner, but with a relaxed presentation and a simple balance of flavors, and always reflective of the season and the garden.

For Ryan, time off to relax is a day visiting the local farms, artisans, and producers and bringing his findings home to his wife and reveling in her excitement. A game of golf is his greatest destresser and, for the ultimate in pampering, he enjoys a massage with his wife and a glass of champagne.

PHIL HUETTENHAIN, VINTAGE 1870 WINE CELLAR, AND THE WINE MATCHER FOR OUR RECIPES

Phil Huettenhain first visited Yountville as a young university student from Chico State as an alternative to his usual trips to Mexico. It was a life-changing experience for Phil. He was so taken by this new world of wine tasting that he returned to his fraternity house with a case of fine wine, much to the shock of his beer-quaffing housemates.

Since that time his passion for wine has grown into a career. After dabbling in a business and marketing career, he gave up a great job, got in his car, and drove back to Napa where he found work in a wine tasting room. And he has never looked back.

Yountville awakened Phil to the world of cuisine and the synergy of food and wine. He realized that living in Yountville and owning the Wine Cellar was more than a career choice. It was a life choice, with the close-knit community, beautiful views, and proximity of many fine restaurants. And it was a town where his business could thrive, from both the locals as well as a large tourist trade. He finds that Yountville brings clients from around the world to his door because of the town's reputation.

Phil loves that the buyers who visit his store keep him professionally challenged. He stays at the forefront of the industry, always broadening his knowledge of varietals from around the world, and has grown to be an expert at giving advice on pairing wine with food. He is often called on to choose wines for menus and events and to speak at seminars. His greatest joy comes from sending a customer away happy, excited, and better educated, or demystifying the wine experience for a new wine buyer. And to help achieve this, he and his staff personally taste all the wines that come into the store. Always one to recognize the team, Phil is quick to acknowledge that it would have been a much harder job without Kevin, his backbone, and the female "superior" palate of the store, Beth.

One of Phil's greatest pleasures is to go home and cook a replica of a dish he has recently enjoyed at a local restaurant, but his ultimate relaxation is to sit on the store's veranda with a glass of Pinot Noir, looking at the surrouding panorama and just taking it all in.

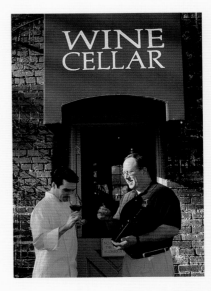

Ryan Jackson and Phil Huettenhain share a glass of wine outside the Vintage 1870 Wine Cellar.

BOB HURLEY, HURLEY'S RESTAURANT AND BAR

Bob Hurley is a man of opposites in balance. He is a warm, easy-going family man who knows how to let loose and go wild. He is also a man of serious reflection who finds laughter in the most demanding situations of life.

Two things made Bob Hurley turn down a fantastic opportunity in Sedona, Arizona, and remain in Yountville. First, he found himself constantly using the locale of Yountville as the benchmark for judging Sedona. Then, the final push came at a fund-raising event for his good friend (and now his general manager) Jerry Lampe, where Bob gave a tribute. He found himself looking at a sea of faces of his friends and colleagues, people who had given him their respect, their hearts, and their appetites. He knew this was too special to give away and decided to open Hurley's Restaurant and Bar.

The laid-back, unpretentious atmosphere of this town was the perfect match for both the Hurley family lifestyle and Bob's style of cooking. Here his kids can walk to school in safety, and people from a range of backgrounds mingle peacefully and with relaxed sophistication.

Bob describes his food as "wine country cooking," reflecting the tone of the Napa Valley—relaxed, simple, uncontrived, and fresh, yet with savoir faire. Bob adheres to tried-and-true techniques while adding fresh Hurley approaches and always focusing on the bounty of the season. His goal is to see that all his diners feel relaxed, pampered, and nourished—and, of course, that they return.

Bob's ultimate therapy is camping next to a pristine river. Add to that dinner at home with his family, a day of focused activity such as fly-fishing, a workout at the local gym, and a stroll through the town's farmers' market and you have the Hurley recipe for total health.

Grape and Almond Gazpacho

BOB HURLEY
HURLEY'S RESTAURANT
AND BAR

On a hot summer day, there's nothing nicer than sitting outside on the patio at Hurley's to watch Yountville life go by while enjoying this stunning gazpacho. It arrives in bowls sitting inside another bowl of ice, and the flavors are refreshing yet deliciously creamy. The crunch and toastiness of the almonds are a delightful finish—and another sign of Bob's playfulness with food textures and flavors while keeping the focus simple.

SERVES 8

2 pounds seedless green grapes

1 cucumber, peeled and chopped

2 tablespoons chopped fresh dill

6 green onions, white and green parts, minced

1 cup plain yogurt

2 tablespoons cream cheese

1 pint milk or half-and-half

$1/4$ cup rice wine vinegar

2 tablespoons light olive oil

Salt and freshly ground white pepper

Cayenne pepper

1 bunch chives, chopped, for garnish

$1/3$ cup toasted slivered almonds, for garnish (see note)

Place the grapes, cucumber, dill, green onions, yogurt, cream cheese, milk, vinegar, and olive oil in a food processor, and process until well blended. Season to taste with salt, white pepper, and cayenne. Chill the soup for at least 1 hour. Serve chilled in soup bowls, garnished with the chives and almonds.

Note: To toast the almonds, place them in a skillet over medium-high heat. Toss them continuously in the skillet until they begin to turn a light golden color. Transfer the almonds to a plate and spread them out in a single layer to cool.

CLASSIC: SPARKLING BLANC DE BLANCS
ADVENTUROUS: OFF-DRY RIESLING (0.5-1.5% RESIDUAL SUGAR)

MARI JENNINGS
GORDON'S CAFÉ &
WINE BAR

SERVES 4 TO 6

4 pounds sweet, red cherry
  tomatoes, stems removed
  (or 3 pounds vine-ripened
  tomatoes, stems removed)

1 English cucumber, coarsely
  chopped

1 yellow or orange bell pepper,
  stemmed, seeded, ribbed, and
  coarsely chopped

1/2 cup loosely packed fresh basil
  leaves

1/2 cup loosely packed fresh
  tarragon leaves

2 bunches chives, chopped

3 tablespoons sherry vinegar

Salt and freshly ground pepper

1/4 cup extra virgin olive oil,
  for garnish

Diced tomatoes, for garnish

Chopped fresh basil, tarragon,
  or chives, for garnish

Mari's Chilled Cherry Tomato Gazpacho

For a more traditional gazpacho, we turn to Mari Jennings of Gordon's. The restaurant's owner, Sally Gordon, swears by Mari's gazpacho, putting it down to her perfect sense of balance of ingredients and her philosophy of paying homage to the bounty of the season. Mari emphasizes that in seemingly simple recipes like this one, every flavor is important, so be sure to choose the best produce available and high-quality sherry vinegar and extra virgin olive oil. At Gordon's, you'll receive this soup served in clear glass bowls that show off the color to its true advantage.

Place the tomatoes, cucumbers, and bell peppers in a food processor, and process until well blended. Add the herbs and vinegar and process until smooth. Season to taste with salt and pepper. Strain the mixture through a medium-mesh sieve, discarding the solids. Chill 15 minutes before serving. Just before serving, drizzle the olive oil over the gazpacho, and mix well. Serve in soup bowls or glasses of choice, garnished with the chopped tomatoes and herbs.

CLASSIC: SAUVIGNON BLANC
ADVENTUROUS: DRY SPARKLING BLANC DE BLANCS

MARI JENNINGS, GORDON'S CAFÉ & WINE BAR

Mari Jennings and Sally Gordon (the café's owner) have what many would say is the perfect business partnership. Together, they have built this very popular and comfortable eatery to what it is today. Sally is the greeting warmth that permeates the space and Mari is the creative zeal behind the food. It was Mari who inspired Sally to add a new dimension to the café with Friday night dinners featuring seasonal produce and wine pairings.

Mari has brought a wealth of experience to Gordon's, from Bistro Don Giovanni, Scala's, Mustards, Foothill Café, and catering on her own. She is a firm believer in keeping food as simple and focused as possible, using what is grown locally and making everything from scratch. Their huge ovens are constantly emanating the aromas of roasting meats and vegetables and rustic desserts and pastries, and the effect is almost hypnotic. One obvious sign is the line waiting at the door for Sunday brunch!

The whole atmosphere of Gordon's reflects the radiance and happy nature of this team and their staff, and the hum of contented diners at the communal and individual tables is enticing. Mari thrives on this positive flow of energy from their customers and finds the small-town feel mirrored in the café very conducive to cooking her style of food.

To wind down, Mari goes for long walks by the vineyards or goes bike riding with her daughter. She loves the refreshing and reviving feeling from a salt soak with essential oils and makes her own blend with Epsom salts, rosemary, and eucalyptus.

Pumpkin and Apple Soup

SERVES 4 TO 6

1 tablespoon extra virgin olive oil

1/2 cup macadamia nuts, coarsely chopped

1 small white onion, chopped

1 teaspoon peeled, grated fresh ginger

3 cups pumpkin, peeled and diced

1 Granny Smith or other tart apple, peeled, cored, and chopped

3 cups chicken stock (page 23)

Salt and pepper

Plain yogurt or crème fraîche, for garnish

2 tablespoons coarsely chopped toasted macadamia nuts, for garnish (see note)

Note: To toast the macadamias, place them in a skillet over medium-high heat. Toss them continuously in the skillet until they begin to turn a light golden color. Transfer the macadamias to a plate and spread them out in a single layer to cool.

Just before Halloween, fields around Yountville can be seen dotted with an array of pumpkins. You can use any pumpkin or winter squash for this recipe. I like to use Japanese (kabocha), Chinese, golden acorn, or other similar round pumpkins for an earthy, rich, home-style flavor. If you use butternut squash, you'll get a sweeter, milder flavor. Macadamia nuts add a richness and nutty texture, and they also thicken the soup without the need for any fats or heavy cream. Although they're often thought of as unhealthy, macadamia nuts are actually high in monounsaturated fat, the same kind as in olive oil.

Heat the olive oil in a large, heavy saucepan over medium heat. Add the 1/2 cup of nuts, the onion, and ginger, and sauté until the mixture is golden brown, 2 to 3 minutes. Add the pumpkin and apple, and sauté for 2 to 3 minutes. Add the stock, cover with a lid, and simmer for about 20 minutes, until the pumpkin is soft. Transfer the mixture to a food processor or blender and process until smooth. Pour the soup back into the pan and reheat. Season with salt and pepper to taste. Serve warm in large bowls, garnished with a dollop of plain yogurt and a sprinkling of the chopped toasted nuts.

CLASSIC: GEWÜRZTRAMINER
ADVENTUROUS: PINOT NOIR

White Bean Minestrone with Garlic and Parmesan Bruschetta

Parmesan Bruschetta

3 thick slices sourdough or rye
  bread
Extra virgin olive oil or lemon-
  infused olive oil, for brushing
1 clove garlic, halved
1 tablespoon grated lemon zest
1 tablespoon freshly grated Parmesan cheese

White Bean Minestrone

1 tablespoon extra virgin olive oil
1 clove garlic, peeled and chopped
1 onion, diced
2 tablespoons fresh thyme leaves
2 stalks celery, finely diced
2 carrots, peeled and finely diced
2 tablespoons tomato paste
4 to 6 cups water
4 ounces dried pasta shells or
  macaroni
2 zucchini, diced
1 cup peeled, diced pumpkin or
  butternut squash
3 Roma tomatoes, peeled, seeded,
  and diced
1/4 cup chopped fresh basil
1 (14-ounce) can white beans or
  cannellini beans, drained
Salt and freshly ground black
  pepper

Freshly grated Parmesan cheese,
  for garnish

In this rendition of classic minestrone soup, I purée half the beans to give the soup a creamy, rich texture. This recipe lends itself well to improvisation, so try any of your favorite vegetables in season, such as broccoli, cauliflower, leeks, or artichokes. Served with the bruschetta, it's the perfect Sunday night meal to enjoy with a movie.

To prepare the bruschetta, preheat oven to 350°F.

Brush the bread slices with olive oil and rub with the cut garlic. Place the slices on a baking sheet and sprinkle with the lemon zest and Parmesan. Bake for 5 minutes, until golden brown and crisp. Cut diagonally into quarters and keep warm until ready to use.

To prepare the minestrone, heat the olive oil in a large, heavy saucepan over medium-high heat, add the garlic and onion, and sauté until soft, 2 to 3 minutes. Add the thyme, celery, and carrots, and sauté 3 minutes longer. Add the tomato paste and cook until the paste starts to deepen in color, about 2 minutes. Add enough of the water to cover the vegetables and bring to a boil. Decrease the heat and simmer until the vegetables are tender, 15 to 20 minutes. Add the pasta, zucchini, and pumpkin, and cook until the pasta is tender, about 10 minutes. Add the tomatoes, basil, and half of the beans, and mix well. Place the remaining beans, along with a few spoonfuls of the soup mixture, in a food processor or blender, and purée. Add the puréed beans to the soup and cook over medium heat until heated through. Season to taste with salt and pepper. Ladle the soup into bowls and garnish with a sprinkling of Parmesan. Serve with the warm bruschetta.

CLASSIC: PINOT GRIGIO
ADVENTUROUS: PINOT NOIR

Cream of Artichoke Soup
with Lemon Pesto

Fresh artichokes have a delicate creamy texture that is just perfect as a base for soup. Before cooking, cut artichokes can quickly turn brown, so have a bowl of lemon water on hand. Immediately after cutting them and removing the chokes, put them in the water, and they'll stay nice and fresh until you are ready to cook them. If you can't find artichokes or if they are out of season, you can use canned artichokes for this recipe. Just rinse them well, and then add them to the simmering stock and potatoes for the last 5 minutes of cooking.

To prepare the soup, trim the leaves and stems from the artichokes. Cut the hearts into quarters and remove the choke. Place the artichokes in a large bowl of water with the lemon slices; set aside.

Heat the olive oil in a large saucepan over medium heat until hot. Add the leek and sauté for 1 minute. Drain the artichokes and pat dry with paper towels. Place the artichokes and potatoes in the pan and sauté for 1 to 2 minutes. Add the herbs, stock, and wine, and bring to a boil. Decrease the heat, cover with a lid, and simmer until the vegetables are tender, 10 to 15 minutes.

Meanwhile, to prepare the pesto, place the basil, lemon juice and zest, almonds, olive oil, and Parmesan in a blender, and process to a coarse paste. Set aside.

To finish the soup, transfer it to a food processor or blender and process until smooth, adding a bit of stock or wine if the soup is too thick. Return the soup to the saucepan and stir in the buttermilk. Gently reheat the soup over low heat, but don't let it boil.

Serve the soup warm, topped with a dollop of the pesto.

CLASSIC: GEWÜRZTRAMINER
ADVENTUROUS: SANGIOVESE

SERVES 4

Soup

4 globe artichokes

1 lemon, sliced

1 tablespoon extra virgin olive oil

1 small leek, rinsed well and sliced

2 medium potatoes, peeled and diced

1 teaspoon fresh oregano leaves

1 teaspoon fresh thyme leaves

2 cups chicken stock (page 23)

1/4 cup dry white wine

1/2 cup buttermilk or milk

Pesto

2 cups loosely packed basil leaves

Juice and grated zest of 1/2 lemon

1/4 cup blanched almonds or cashews

2 tablespoons extra virgin olive oil

1 tablespoon freshly grated Parmesan cheese

Stocks

Making your own stock may seem time-consuming, especially with the range of tasty liquid free-range and organic products now available in stores. However, there's nothing quite like the flavor of homemade broth, and you know exactly what's in it!

STRAINING AND STORING

When preparing stock to store, strain the hot stock through a sieve lined with cheesecloth into a stainless steel bowl. Place the bowl in iced water and stir occasionally while cooling. Stock can be stored, covered, in the refrigerator for 2 to 3 days or frozen for 2 to 3 months (2 to 3 weeks for fish stock). For convenience, once the stock has been strained, return it to the saucepan and simmer until the mixture is reduced to about a quarter of its original volume to concentrate the flavors. Freeze in ice cube trays and add to dishes as you would bouillon cubes.

Vegetable Stock

MAKES ABOUT 8 CUPS

3 teaspoons olive oil
1 onion, diced
2 stalks celery, with leaves, chopped
2 carrots, sliced
1 small leek, washed and sliced
1/2 cup sliced mushrooms, optional
10 to 12 cups cold water
2 sprigs fresh parsley
1 sprig fresh thyme
1 clove
10 black peppercorns
Salt

Vegetable stock is a great alternative to chicken stock, and adds flavor and depth to soups, casseroles, and sauces.

Heat the olive oil in a large stockpot. Add the onion and sauté over medium heat until soft. Add the celery, carrots, leek, and mushrooms and sauté for 2 minutes, stirring constantly. Add the water, parsley, thyme, clove, peppercorns, and salt to taste and bring to a boil. Decrease the heat and simmer, uncovered, for 45 minutes, skimming the surface. Strain the stock as described in the instructions above. Discard the contents of the sieve. Allow the stock to cool completely before storing in a covered container in the refrigerator.

Chicken Stock

The most universally popular stock for a realm of cuisines, home-made chicken stock is a great basis for sauces, soups, stews, and risotto.

Rinse the chicken bones under cold running water and place in a large stock pot. Add the water and bring to a boil over high heat. Decrease the heat and simmer for 1 hour, skimming the surface as needed. Add the vegetables, herbs, and seasonings, and simmer for another hour. Add a little more water during the cooking to maintain the volume. Strain the stock as described in the instructions on page 22. Discard the contents of the sieve. Allow the stock to cool completely before storing in a covered container in the refrigerator. Once the stock is chilled, remove the solidified fat from the top.

MAKES ABOUT 8 CUPS

2 pounds chicken bones, skin and
    fat removed
10 to 12 cups water
1 carrot, chopped
1 onion, chopped
1 stalk celery, with leaves, chopped
Pinch of salt
2 to 3 sprigs parsley
1 sprig thyme
1 bay leaf
10 black peppercorns

Fish Stock

Fish stock is wonderfully flavorful and great for poaching fish, making seafood-based soups and sauces, as well as adding to stir fries and pasta or rice dishes. For an Asian twist, add a stalk of crushed lemongrass, a kaffir lime leaf, and some fresh ginger or galangal.

Rinse the fish bones under cold running water and remove any blood, gills, or dark skin. In a large stock pot, heat the oil to medium-high. Combine the fish bones, leek, celery, and carrot in the stock pot and sauté for 2 to 3 minutes, until the leek is soft but not browned. Add the mushrooms, herbs, water, wine, and salt to taste and bring to a boil. Decrease the heat and simmer for 20 to 25 minutes, skimming the foam as necessary. Strain the stock as described in the instructions on page 22. Discard the contents of the sieve. Return the stock to a clean saucepan. Simmer for 10 more minutes to concentrate the flavors.

MAKES ABOUT 4 CUPS

1 pound fish bones and/or prawn
    shells (avoid fresh water fish
    or salmon)
1 teaspoon olive or peanut oil
1 leek
1 stalk celery, chopped
1 carrot, chopped
1/2 cup chopped mushrooms
1 teaspoon black peppercorns
1 sprig thyme or oregano
2 sprigs parsley
4 to 5 cups water
1 cup dry white wine
Salt

Salads and Vegetables

Fricassee of Summer Sweet Onions with Périgord Truffles and Truffle Glace, page 26

SERVES 4

Onion Vinaigrette

1 tablespoon unsalted butter
1 tablespoon plus ¹/₂ cup grape-
    seed oil
2 medium white onions, quartered
2 cups vegetable stock (page 22)
2 cups water
1 teaspoon sherry vinegar
Kosher salt
Freshly ground black pepper

Summer Sweet Onion Fricassee

8 white pearl onions, peeled
8 cipollini onions, peeled
2 teaspoons white truffle oil
2 sprigs thyme
Kosher salt
Freshly ground black pepper
2 tablespoons unsalted butter
2 tablespoons granulated sugar
¹/₂ cup water
8 red pearl onions, peeled
2 scallions, blanched (see note), cut
    diagonally into ¹/₂-inch slices
1 tablespoon chopped black
    Périgord truffles

Fricassee of Summer Sweet Onions with Périgord Truffles and Truffle Glace

Anyone who has been fortunate enough to dine at Thomas Keller's French Laundry in Yountville will appreciate his talent for using the finest quality ingredients and turning them into small taste sensations. The flavors are focused, intense enough to stimulate the palate, yet leave you with an exquisite sense of longing. That's exactly how I felt when I tasted this dish. Enjoy his creation in your own home and savor it slowly—you will enjoy every creative minute you spend in the kitchen as much as you will eating it. Part of the fricassee recipe involves a cooking method known as sous vide, or "with vacuum." This relatively new method involves combining and cooking ingredients in vacuum-packed pouches, and it is becoming more and more common in kitchens around the world. The special bags are now available in many gourmet kitchenware stores, but you can also use medium-size heavy-duty zip-top bags instead.

To make the vinaigrette, heat the butter and 1 tablespoon of the grapeseed oil in a large sauté pan over medium heat. Once the butter is melted, add the onions and slowly cook, stirring, until lightly caramelized and golden brown. Add the stock and water, and simmer until the stock is infused with the flavor of the caramelized onions, about 30 minutes. Strain the liquid through a fine-mesh sieve into a small saucepan, discarding the solids. Add the sherry vinegar and slowly reduce over medium-low heat until about ¹/₂ cup of liquid remains. Strain the vinaigrette again into a small bowl, cover with plastic wrap, and refrigerate for several hours until chilled. Once chilled, remove and discard the butter that has solidified on top. While whisking, slowly add the remaining ¹/₂ cup of grapeseed oil, and whisk until smooth. Season to taste with kosher salt and freshly ground black pepper. Set aside at room temperature until ready to use.

To make the fricassee, fill a large stockpot about three-quarters full with water and bring to a rolling boil over high heat. Meanwhile, fill 1 vacuum bag with the white pearl onions and another with the cipollini onions. In each bag, place one teaspoon of white truffle oil, one sprig of thyme, and a pinch of kosher salt and pepper to taste. Seal the bags, releasing the air.

Once the water comes to a boil, place the sealed bags in the pot and cover with a plate to hold them under the water. Boil for 5 to 7 minutes, until the onions feel tender to the touch through the bag. Remove the bags from the water and set aside until ready to use.

Heat the butter, sugar, a pinch of salt, and the water in a small saucepan over medium heat, until the butter is melted. Mix well, then add the red pearl onions and slowly simmer over low heat until they are cooked through and are well coated with the glaze, 10 to 15 minutes. Set aside until ready to use.

To make the truffle glace, combine the truffle juice, truffle vinegar, and sugar in a small saucepan over medium-high heat, and reduce just until the mixture coats the back of the spoon. (If the mixture reduces too much, it will become bitter, so be careful.) Remove the pan from the heat.

To finish the dish, open the 2 vacuum-packed bags and pour the contents into a small saucepan. Add the glazed red pearl onions and the scallions, chopped truffles, and the onion vinaigrette. Place the pan over medium heat and cook until just heated through. Season to taste with kosher salt and freshly ground black pepper.

To serve, divide the fricassee among four plates. Drizzle a little of the truffle glace around each plate, sprinkle with a pinch of fleur de sel, and garnish with chopped chives.

Note: Black truffle juice is the remaining liquid from boiled truffles. It's very popular with chefs as a flavoring for pasta, rice, sauces, and dressing, and can be obtained online from trufflemarket.com or ask your local specialty food store.

Note: To blanch the scallions, place them in a large pot of salted, boiling water and cook until tender. The scallion leaves will be soft and pliable when done. The white parts will also be soft and translucent when done. Remove the scallions from the pot, and immediately plunge them into a large pot of ice water until chilled. Drain and use as directed.

Truffle Glace

1 cup black truffle juice (see note)

1/2 cup truffle-infused vinegar (available at many specialty food stores)

1/4 cup granulated sugar

Kosher salt
Freshly ground black pepper
Fleur de sel (sea salt), for garnish
Chopped fresh chives, for garnish

WINE PAIRING BY THE FRENCH LAUNDRY SOMMELIER
DOMAINE ZIND HUMBRECHT "CLOS WINDSBUHL" 1999
PINOS GRIS. THIS IS AN OFF-DRY PINOT GRIS FROM ALSACE, FRANCE.

THOMAS KELLER, THE FRENCH LAUNDRY

Thomas Keller lives The French Laundry, breathes The French Laundry, nurtures and tends The French Laundry. It was what brought this esteemed chef to Yountville. To him the corner was magical and he found himself emotionally connected to the history, charm, and character of the building, which has become like family to him.

Into its walls he has built his own style of cuisine and service, and the building has evolved with his vision and that unique Thomas Keller touch. Into its gardens he has brought seasonal produce for his restaurant, giving his chefs a true respect for the ingredients they cook with. From planting and tending the seedlings and learning when to harvest to capture the best flavor, to seeing them to their exquisite completeness on plates.

What is Keller's cuisine? It's more of a philosophy—of minimalism, of a heightened sense of flavor, of small courses designed to tease the palate with impact and build growing anticipation for what is to come rather than simply providing satiety. It's about every mouthful being so delectable that the sense of lingering is extreme.

Like the building blocks of his dishes, Thomas also takes care of himself with a regular workout and a massage when he has time. And when he has a chance to get out, he reflects on one thing he loves about being in Yountville—he can go for a burger at Mustards, pasta at Piatti, a margarita at Compadres, or a late night snack and wine amid friends at Bouchon, relax in the comfort and ambience of Bistro Jeanty's bar, or just enjoy some rustic bread or an ice cream at Bouchon Bakery—and never have to get in a car.

Roasted Mixed Potato and Arugula Salad

Roasting root vegetables brings out their earthy, rich flavors. Served either warm or cold on a bed of crisp, peppery arugula with splash of red wine vinaigrette, they transform into a delicious salad. Here, I've added a scattering of feta cheese and toasted pine nuts to add texture and variety. This hearty salad is especially satisfying with some crusty Italian or rye bread.

To cook the potatoes and yams, preheat the oven to 400°F. Place the potatoes and yams on a baking sheet and toss with olive oil to coat. Cook for 30 to 40 minutes, stirring occasionally, until tender. Remove from the oven and allow to cool.

To prepare the vinaigrette, whisk together all the ingredients a medium bowl.

To serve, combine the leek and arugula in a large bowl, and toss with the vinaigrette. Place the greens on a serving platter or divide among individual plates. Top with the vegetables and scatter the feta and pine nuts over the top. Serve immediately.

Note: To toast the pine nuts, place the nuts in a skillet over medium-high heat. Toss them continuously in the skillet until they begin to turn a light golden color. Transfer the pine nuts to a plate and spread them out in a single layer to cool.

CLASSIC: MERLOT
ADVENTUROUS: GEWÜRZTRAMINER

SERVES 6 TO 8

1 pound yams or sweet potatoes, scrubbed and cut into 1/2-inch dice

1 pound russet, fingerling, black, or other potatoes, scrubbed and cut into 1/2-inch dice

Olive oil

Red Wine Vinaigrette

1 tablespoon red wine vinegar or balsamic vinegar

2 tablespoons extra virgin olive oil

Juice and zest of 1/2 orange

2 teaspoons Dijon mustard

Freshly ground black pepper

1 leek, rinsed well and thinly sliced

2 bunches arugula, rinsed well, dried, and roughly chopped

1/4 cup crumbled feta cheese

2 to 3 tablespoons toasted pine nuts (see note)

SERVES 8

Marinated Beets

3 pounds beets, trimmed and
    peeled
1/4 cup sherry vinegar
1/3 cup extra virgin olive oil
1/2 to 1 teaspoon salt
1 teaspoon freshly ground black
    pepper

Citrus Dressing

Juice of 6 oranges
Juice of 2 lemons
Juice of 1 lime
1-inch piece of peeled, fresh ginger,
    sliced
2 tablespoons sherry vinegar
1/2 to 1 cup olive oil
Salt and freshly ground black pepper

6 to 8 ounces mâche lettuce, rinsed
    well and dried
32 orange segments (about 4 to
    6 oranges)
8 ounces feta cheese
Freshly ground black pepper

Beet and Mâche Salad with Feta Cheese and Citrus Dressing

Whenever I enjoy a meal surrounded by the French country décor and atmosphere of Bistro Jeanty, I order this salad. Its simple flavors blend together like French champagne and romance, and whet your appetite for the outstanding food that follows. Keep in mind that the beets need to marinate for at least six hours, so plan on starting this step early in the day or even the night before. The dressing will probably be more than you'll need for this salad, but it's great to have on hand for salads over the next few days.

To prepare the beets, place them in a large saucepan, add enough water to cover, and bring to a boil over high heat. Decrease the heat and simmer until tender when pierced, about 25 to 30 minutes. Drain well, let cool completely, and dice. In a medium bowl, combine the vinegar, olive oil, salt, and pepper. Add 4 cups of the beets (reserve any extras for another use) and mix well. Cover with plastic wrap and refrigerate for at least 6 hours or overnight.

To make the dressing, combine the orange, lemon, and lime juices, ginger, and vinegar in a nonreactive pan over high heat and bring to a boil. Decrease the heat to a simmer and reduce the mixture until syrupy. Remove the pan from the heat and let cool. While whisking, slowly add the olive oil to taste. Season to taste with salt and pepper.

To assemble the salad, divide the beets among individual bowls, mounding them in the center of the bowls. Distribute the lettuce over the beets. Randomly place the orange segments around the outside of the beets. Crumble the feta cheese over the top of the salads, being careful not to crush the lettuce. Drizzle with the dressing and finish with freshly ground black pepper to taste.

CLASSIC: PROSECCO
ADVENTUROUS: SPARKLING WINE

PHILIPPE JEANTY, BISTRO JEANTY

"It's like being in a small French country town without being in France," says the consummate French gentleman who has helped shape the face of what Yountville is today.

Arriving in a very different, bar-dominated town in 1977, the young and eager Philippe Jeanty saw the potential of Yountville and recognized the great opportunity it offered him. And indeed his vision has come into fruition as he brings a taste of the French countryside to contented diners.

Philippe has captured the rural small-town atmosphere in his restaurant and the food is the perfect fit—what he describes as French "soul" food in a bistro-style setting. He loves the fact that this valley allows him to be friends with the local winemakers and chefs and that life is not work, it's a lifestyle.

In Yountville he has been able to pursue his dream and has been willing to work hard to get there. All he missed from France was the history and architecture. So, when he finally purchased the historical building and restaurant once called Jack's (now Jeanty at Jack's) in nearby San Francisco, he really feels he has all life can offer.

To keep this energetic and radiant chef up to speed with life's demands, he is often seen on the streets of Yountville on morning walks or bike riding. His favorite way to destress is to go home to his family, pour a glass of wine, and read a book. "And all I have to do when I'm feeling like a real break is walk across the road to Villagio Spa for a few days of massages and relaxing by the pool, and I feel like I've been on a week-long holiday without having to fly anywhere."

What more could a Frenchman want?

Baby Spinach, Pear, and Fennel Salad with Toasted Pecans

As the weather begins to take on a crisp chill in fall, local farmers begin turning out pears, apples, and other orchard fruits. They make great additions to salads and, sometimes, for a warm, "comfort salad," I like to roast the fruit slices first in a little white wine in a moderate oven for 5 to 7 minutes and toss them, while still warm, with the greens.

In a medium bowl, toss the pears with the fennel. In a small bowl, whisk together the goat cheese, buttermilk, olive oil, truffle oil, and lemon juice and zest, and pour over the pear and fennel mixture. To serve, place the spinach in a serving bowl and top with the pear and fennel mixture. Sprinkle with the toasted pecans. Serve immediately, with the bread and a small bowl of olive oil for dipping on the side.

Note: To toast the pecans, place the nuts in a skillet over medium-high heat. Toss them continuously in the skillet until they begin to turn a light golden color. Transfer the pecans to a plate and spread them out in a single layer to cool.

CLASSIC: PINOT GRIGIO
ADVENTUROUS: A LIGHT MERLOT

SERVES 6

3 pears, such as Bosc, Red Sensation, or Nashi, or a combination, cored and thinly sliced

1 small bulb fennel, white part only, sliced

2 tablespoons soft goat cheese

2 tablespoons buttermilk

1 tablespoon extra virgin olive oil

A few drops truffle- or lemon-infused olive oil

Juice and zest of 1/2 lemon

10 to 12 ounces baby spinach leaves

1/3 cup chopped toasted pecans (see note)

1 loaf Pugliese or other rustic Italian bread

Extra virgin olive oil for dipping

Warm Roasted Mushroom and Feta Salad

4 cups mixed mushrooms, such as cremini, shiitake, and oyster

1/2 red onion, finely diced

4 cups mixed baby Asian greens, such as mizuna or tatsoi, or curly endive

1/3 cup crumbled feta cheese

1/3 cup chopped toasted pecans, walnuts, or pine nuts (see note)

2 tablespoons extra virgin olive oil

1 tablespoon freshly squeezed lemon juice

1 teaspoon Dijon or horseradish mustard

Salt and freshly ground black pepper

Note: To toast the nuts, place them in a skillet over medium-high heat. Toss them continuously in the skillet until they begin to turn a light golden color. Transfer the nuts to a plate and spread them out in a single layer to cool.

This is one of my favorite salad appetizers for a cool winter night. Roasting mushrooms brings out their earthy and woody flavors, and it also sends some tantalizing aromas through the kitchen. To prepare the mushrooms, it's best to clean them with just a damp paper towel, and to roast them in a rimmed pan that will catch all the juices. You can either use mixed Asian greens for this dish or choose your own selection.

To prepare the salad, preheat the oven to 350°F. Line a baking sheet or other large rimmed pan with parchment paper or foil, making sure to cover the pan completely and over the rim so it catches all the juices from the mushrooms.

Place the mushrooms in a single layer on the prepared pan. Bake for 15 to 20 minutes, until they have started to soften and lose their juices. Carefully tip the pan to pour the liquid into a bowl; set aside. Let the mushrooms cool slightly, then chop into bite-sized pieces. In a medium bowl, toss the mushrooms with the red onion.

To serve, divide the greens among the plates and top with the warm mushrooms. Scatter the feta and pecans over the mushrooms. Add the olive oil, lemon juice, and mustard to the reserved mushroom juice, mix well, and season to taste with salt and pepper. Drizzle over the salads and serve immediately.

CLASSIC: PINOT GRIGIO
ADVENTUROUS: PINOT NOIR

Grilled Asparagus and Goat Cheese Bruschetta

Locally produced goat's milk cheese is readily available around the Napa Valley from farmers who have mastered the art. With its ripe, tart flavor, goat cheese makes a perfect match for the grassy flavor of fresh asparagus, especially when finished with a scattering of earthy roasted hazelnuts.

To prepare the dressing, combine the balsamic vinegar, lemon juice, olive oil, and dill in a small bowl, and mix well; set aside.

To prepare the bruschetta, oil and preheat a grill pan over medium-high heat. Place the asparagus on the grill pan, and grill for 1 to 2 minutes, turning the asparagus once or twice, just until crisp-tender. Transfer to a plate and set aside. Place the bread slices on the grill pan, and grill until lightly browned on each side. Remove from the grill and immediately spread each slice with some of the goat cheese.

To serve, place the bruschetta on a serving platter, top each slice with 4 spears of the warm asparagus, and drizzle with the dressing. Sprinkle with the hazelnuts and season with cracked pepper. Serve warm.

CLASSIC: SAUVIGNON BLANC
ADVENTUROUS: RISKY, BUT TRY A SANGIOVESE (100%)

SERVES 4

Dressing

1 tablespoon balsamic vinegar
Juice of 1/2 lemon
2 tablespoons extra virgin olive oil
1 tablespoon chopped fresh dill
  or basil

16 spears fresh asparagus, ends
  trimmed
4 thick slices Pugliese, ciabatta, or
  sourdough bread
4 to 6 tablespoons soft goat
  cheese or ricotta cheese
2 to 3 tablespoons chopped
  roasted hazelnuts (optional)
Freshly cracked black pepper

SERVES 6

Walnut Vinaigrette

1 tablespoon chopped shallots

1 tablespoon Dijon mustard

1/4 cup red wine vinegar

1 cup olive oil

1/2 cup walnut oil (see note)

Salt and freshly ground black pepper

Raspberry Vinaigrette

1 tablespoon chopped shallots

1/4 cup raspberries

1 tablespoon red wine vinegar

1/2 cup olive oil

Salt and freshly ground black pepper

1 to 2 handfuls loosely packed
   arugula leaves

2 large heads Belgian endive, leaves
   separated

1 small seedless watermelon, cut
   into 1/2-inch dice

1 medium red onion, halved and
   sliced

24 diagonally cut baguette slices,
   lightly toasted

12 ounces goat cheese

6 ounces prosciutto, thinly sliced
   into strips

Chopped fresh chives, for garnish

Watermelon Salad with Prosciutto, Arugula, and Red Onions

This is one of Bob Hurley's fun dishes and features a range of flavors—sweet (watermelon), salty (prosciutto), and bitter (endive). The salad includes both walnut and raspberry vinaigrettes, and since the two recipes yield a bit more than you'll need for the salads, you may want to savor them over another day or two on more salads or even as a dip for bread.

To make the walnut vinaigrette, place the shallots, mustard, and vinegar in food processor or blender and process until well blended. With the motor running, slowly add the olive oil and then the walnut oil, and process until smooth and emulsified. Season to taste with salt and pepper; set aside.

To make the raspberry vinaigrette, place the shallots, raspberries, and vinegar in food processor or blender and process until well blended. With the motor running, slowly add the olive oil and process until smooth and emulsified. Season to taste with salt and pepper; set aside.

To prepare the salad, place the arugula and endive leaves in a large bowl, and toss with enough of the walnut vinaigrette to coat lightly. Arrange the greens around the outer edge of a serving platter. Combine the watermelon and onions in another bowl, and toss with enough of the raspberry vinaigrette to coat the melon. Place the watermelon mixture on the platter in the center of the greens. Spread the toasted baguette slices with the goat cheese, top with prosciutto slices, and arrange in a circle between the watermelon mixture and the greens. Garnish with a sprinkle of chives.

Note: You can buy walnut oil in most supermarkets and specialty food stores. It's a bit expensive, but the flavor is rich and intense and a little goes a long way.

CLASSIC: YOUNG SPARKLING BRUT OR DRY RIESLING
ADVENTUROUS: GRENACHE

Shaved Summer Squash, Watercress, and Chicken Salad with Blue Cheese

JUDE WILMOTH
NAPA VALLEY GRILLE

Jude Wilmoth brings a light, seasonal, and flavorful touch to the menu at the Napa Valley Grille with this summer salad. The fresh garden flavors from the squash and watercress are perfectly finished with a piquant crumbling of moist blue cheese.

In a large bowl, toss together the squash, corn, watercress, and shredded chicken. In a small bowl, whisk together the olive oil and the lemon juice and zest, and season to taste with salt and pepper. Pour the dressing over the salad and toss well. Top with the blue cheese, and serve immediately.

CLASSIC: MARSANNE OR MARSANNE/VIOGNIER BLEND
ADVENTUROUS: LATE HARVEST SAUVIGNON BLANC

SERVES 4

1 zucchini, thinly shaved into strips with a mandoline or a vegetable peeler

1 crookneck squash, thinly shaved into strips with a mandoline or a vegetable peeler

Freshly cut kernels from 3 ears sweet corn

1/2 pound watercress, rinsed well and separated

2 cups shredded roasted chicken

3 tablespoons extra virgin olive oil

Juice and grated zest of 2 lemons

Salt and freshly ground pepper

3 to 4 tablespoons crumbled blue cheese

JUDE WILMOTH, NAPA VALLEY GRILLE

Jude was raised in St. Helena. One of eight children, he was brought up on comfort food, Italian-style living, and growing vegetables in the backyard. His love of food was kindled from an early age with a great influence from his family's friends, the Chiarello family of the famous Tra Vigne restaurant. In fact, his first job was as a busboy at the restaurant. Soon he was working his way up to the pantry before he left to study and cook at different locations to broaden his repertoire.

Jude is a chef with purpose, who loves the whole occasion of food and wine—cooking, eating, crushing grapes, and socializing. His personal preference is for Mediterranean-style food with a light-hand, which he offers at the Grille alongside a rich creamy risotto and other comforting dishes his customers come back for.

Quality of life is important to Jude and he finds being in the Napa Valley allows him to have that. For Jude, quality comes in a relaxing game of golf or a scenic drive up the valley, where he can roll down the windows and smell the grapes being crushed. It comes in his morning runs past the vineyards, when he can meditate and plan his day. Jude's ultimate time-out is to travel to Italy where he has a huge passion for the people, their way of life, and the food. Perhaps that is why he has chosen to stay near Yountville, the town he says is the closest he can come to being in Tuscany, yet still be in the U.S.

Julio Garcia
Pacific Blues Café

❲

SERVES 6 TO 8

Dressing

¹/₄ cup rice vinegar

¹/₄ cup soy sauce

1 to 2 tablespoons sugar

2 tablespoons chopped fresh cilantro

2 tablespoons peeled, chopped fresh ginger

1 tablespoon chopped garlic

¹/₃ cup olive oil

1 teaspoon crushed red pepper flakes

Salad

2 boneless, skinless chicken breasts, cooked, cooled, and shredded

2 heads napa cabbage, shredded

4 carrots, peeled and julienned

6 green onions, white and green parts, chopped

1 cup crispy Chinese noodles, available from most supermarkets and specialty food stores

Spicy Ginger Oriental Salad

One of the institutions of Yountville, Pacific Blues is perhaps best known for its variety of home-style burgers and American food, but most people I know will pick this dish as one of their favorites for enjoying on the deck on a warm sunny day. This salad is also delicious when served topped with grilled salmon or fried calamari.

To prepare the dressing, whisk together all of the dressing ingredients in a large bowl until well blended. To finish the salad, add the chicken, cabbage, carrots, green onions, and noodles, and toss to coat. Serve immediately.

CLASSIC: DRY GEWÜRZTRAMINER
ADVENTUROUS: RED ZINFANDEL

❲

JULIO GARCIA, PACIFIC BLUES CAFÉ

Yountville's culinary reputation reached down to Mexico and Julio was quick to decide that if he was going to pursue his career as a chef, this was where he wanted to be. Coming from working at a small taqueria, his inclination led him to a local Mexican restaurant, where he stayed for eight years. Pacific Blues owner, Jeff Steen, was impressed by the skills of this budding chef and asked him to come and open the café.

Since opening Pacific Blues, Julio and Jeff have allowed the cuisine to evolve, veering from the traditional burger café as they found their diners were more adventurous. This was ideal for Julio, who loves to diverge from the norm and experiment with flavors, especially when he can introduce some of the ingredients and techniques from his Mexican heritage. To be able to put his skills to the test amid the community feel of the café was a dream come true. Locals responded with enthusiasm, enjoying the added spice, which seemed the perfect match for the café's range of beers and local wines. "Maverick American" became a term applied to his cuisine and almost every local you talk to has their favorite at "the Blues."

An active and fit man, Julio rides a bike to work and goes for a regular workout at the gym. He loves to restaurant hop to discover new flavors and bring the ideas home to cook for his wife. To relax, he treats himself to a massage or goes shopping at culinary stores. Julio values the importance of eight hours of sleep a night, believing it's essential to stay on top and give Pacific Blues diners the best he can.

SERVES 4 TO 6

Basil Oil

1/2 cup loosely packed fresh basil
    leaves
1/2 cup extra virgin olive oil
Salt and freshly ground black pepper

Balsamic Glaze

1 cup balsamic vinegar
3 tablespoons sugar
3/4 cup port
1 sprig thyme
2 tablespoons honey

1 to 2 tablespoons extra virgin
    olive oil
2 medium Chinese eggplants, cut
    crosswise into 1/8-inch-thick
    slices
Salt and white pepper
1 cup chicken stock (page 23)
2 tablespoons balsamic vinegar
2 sheets gelatin, or two packages
    unflavored gelatin
8 to 10 large heirloom or vine-
    ripened tomatoes, peeled (see
    note, page 44), quartered, and
    seeded
1 bunch basil leaves
Arugula leaves, for garnish

Heirloom Tomato and Eggplant Terrine

This classy yet simple dish captures the essence of summer. There is nothing more inviting than sitting at Cucina à la Carte on a warm summer afternoon enjoying this light, flavorful dish and a glass of wine.

To make the basil oil, bring a small saucepan of water to a boil over high heat, add the basil, and blanch for 1 minute. Drain immediately, then plunge into a bowl of ice water to shock, or stop the cooking process. Drain well, then use paper towels to squeeze out as much moisture as possible. Place the basil in a food processor with the olive oil and process until smooth. Season to taste with salt and pepper. Strain the mixture through a coffee filter into a small bowl. Cover with plastic wrap and refrigerate until ready to use. (Any leftover basil oil will keep, refrigerated, for up to one week.)

To make the balsamic glaze, place all of the ingredients in a saucepan over high heat and bring to a boil. Decrease the heat to a simmer and reduce the mixture until thick and syrupy, about 10 to 20 minutes. Transfer the glaze to a bowl, let cool, and then refrigerate until ready to use.

To sear the eggplant, heat the olive oil in a sauté pan over high heat until hot. Add the eggplant slices and sear for 1 minute per side, then drain on paper towels. Transfer the eggplant to a baking sheet and season to taste with salt and white pepper.

To prepare the gelatin, place the chicken stock in a saucepan over high heat and bring to a boil. Add the balsamic vinegar and season to taste with salt and white pepper. Add the gelatin, stir to dissolve, and cook just until the mixture comes back to a boil. Strain the mixture through a fine-mesh sieve into a bowl; set aside.

To assemble the terrine, line a terrine pan or small loaf pan with enough plastic wrap to allow you to overlap the top of the filled pan completely. Cover the bottom of the pan with a single layer of the eggplant slices, and brush lightly with the gelatin mixture. Place a single layer of the tomato wedges over the eggplant, season with salt and pepper, then top with a layer of basil leaves. Continue layering the remaining eggplant, gelatin mixture, tomatoes, and basil until the pan is filled to just about 1/4 inch over the top. Fold the plastic wrap over the terrine to cover. Place a cutting board or piece of sturdy cardboard over the top of the terrine, then set a heavy can on top of the board to weigh it down. Refrigerate for at least 10 hours or overnight.

To serve, gently remove the terrine from the pan and unwrap the plastic. Using a long, sharp knife, slice the terrine into 1/2-inch slices.

Divide the arugula among individual plates and top with a slice of terrine. Drizzle the basil oil and balsamic glaze around the arugula. Serve cold.

Note: To blanch and peel the tomatoes, fill a large bowl with water and ice cubes. Bring a large pot of water to a boil. Remove the core from the tomatoes and, using a fork, plunge each tomato into boiling water for 10 seconds then into the iced water to cool. Peel the skin and cut each tomato into four wedges. Remove the seeds and dry the wedges on paper towels.

CLASSIC: SAUVIGNON BLANC
ADVENTUROUS: DRY ROSÉ

STEFAN RICHTER, EXECUTIVE CHEF, VILLAGIO INN & SPA AND CUCINA À LA CARTE

When Stefan Richter arrived in Yountville he found himself, for the first time in his life, thinking, "At last I have found somewhere I want to stay!" And this lively young Finnish chef has worked in many coveted locations around the world.

In Yountville, Stefan has found a career and a life—each of two extremes that can seemingly coexist in unity. At Villagio and its signature restaurant, Stefan's burning desire to be constantly challenged is fulfilled as he weaves his way from designing conference, room service, and spa menus, to preparing a relaxed but inspired menu for the Cucina à la Carte marketplace. He also fulfills his passion of being able to nurture a garden to provide some of the restaurant's produce.

But also in Yountville, with its lush wine country soils, close-knit community, and rural peace, Stefan has found a place where he can still have time with his wife, tend to his own garden, and experience the joy of taking food from the soil to the plate. He can go fishing and have a massage within hours of each other and be back at the property to tend to banquets all within the space of a day.

A man whose life demands a constant supply of high energy, Stefan likes to keep fit with a regular workout in the local gym. He also firmly believes in the therapeutic power of his favorite tonic—a glass of cucumber water with lime and lemon, which he finds both refreshing and reviving.

Mixed Spring Vegetables
with Fava Bean-Fresh Herb Sauce

One of the joys of spring is the start of the farmers' markets that bring us all the glorious produce and flowers of the season. At Yountville's popular farmers' market on Wednesday afternoons, you can wander among the local farmers' stands, choose home-made breads, mustards, and oils, sample wines and locally grown nuts, and buy a bunch of beautiful spring blossoms to take home. This recipe captures some of the flavors from the market, but it can also be made with any of your favorite vegetables in season. The fava beans in the sauce add a smooth, rich texture—but no additional fat—making this a deliciously healthy main dish.

To prepare the vegetables, preheat the oven to 250°F.

In a large saucepan, bring the stock to a boil. Add the leek and fennel, and decrease the heat to a simmer. Cover with a lid and simmer for 6 to 8 minutes, until the fennel is nearly tender. Drain off about one-half of the steaming liquid, reserving it for the sauce, and leave the leek and fennel in the pan. Add the zucchini, squash, corn, and bell pepper to the pan, cover with a lid, and cook for 3 to 4 minutes, until the corn is tender. Add the asparagus and peas, and cook for 1 minute. Remove the pan from the heat. Transfer the vegetables to a baking dish, add the tomatoes and cucumber, and toss well. Drizzle the vegetables with enough of the olive oil to just coat, and season to taste with salt and pepper. Place in the oven to keep warm while you make the sauce.

To prepare the sauce, place the reserved steaming liquid in a saucepan over moderate heat and bring to a simmer. Add the fava beans and simmer for 4 to 5 minutes, until tender. Transfer the beans to a food processor or blender, reserving the liquid. Add the herbs, ricotta cheese, yogurt, and lemon juice, and process until smooth. If the sauce is too thick, add some of the reserved liquid.

To serve, place the vegetable in a serving bowl or on a platter. Spoon the sauce over the warm vegetables, and serve immediately.

CLASSIC: PINOT GRIS

ADVENTUROUS: DRY ROSÉ

SERVES 4 TO 6

- 1 cup chicken (page 23) or vegetable stock (page 22), white wine, or water
- 1 leek, rinsed well and cut crosswise into 1-inch pieces
- 1 bulb fennel, trimmed and cut lengthwise into 6 to 8 wedges
- 1 zucchini, sliced into 1-inch rounds
- 4 to 6 small green or yellow summer squash, quartered
- 1 ear of corn, shucked and cut crosswise into 4 to 6 pieces
- 1 red bell pepper, stemmed, seeded, ribbed, and diced
- 8 asparagus spears, ends trimmed and halved
- 1/2 cup freshly shelled peas
- 1/2 cup cherry tomatoes, stemmed
- 1/2 cucumber, diced
- Extra virgin olive oil
- Salt and freshly ground black pepper

Fava Bean-Fresh Herb Sauce

- 1 cup freshly shelled fava beans
- 1/2 cup loosely packed fresh mixed herbs, such as mint, basil, parsley, and cilantro
- 2 tablespoons ricotta cheese
- 2 tablespoons plain yogurt
- 1 tablespoon freshly squeezed lemon juice

Freeform Cherry Tomato and Cannellini Tarts with Pine Nut Pastry

Inspired by the bountiful cherry tomatoes available throughout the summer, I created this tart recipe that combines the bright, piquant flavor of tomatoes with the smooth richness of bean purée. Making the pastry from pine nuts not only makes it a healthier and lighter pastry, it also adds a delightful crunch and nutty flavor. Don't worry about cutting the pastry into perfect shapes—that's why they're called "freeform"!

To make the pastry, place the pine nuts and flour in a food processor, and process just until the nuts begin to break up. While pulsing the processor on and off, gradually add the oil and then the milk, pulsing just until the mixture comes together into a dough. Transfer to a floured board and knead gently until smooth. Wrap the dough in plastic wrap and refrigerate for 30 minutes.

Preheat the oven to 350°F. Lightly oil a baking sheet.

On a sheet of parchment paper or a well-floured board, roll out the pastry into about a 12 by 16-inch rectangle about 1/4 inch thick. Cut the dough into 4 to 6 squares. Lightly brush the edges of each square with water, then fold in the edges about 1/2 inch. Make another 1/2 inch fold along the edges, pinching the corners and pressing the edges to make a rim. Lift the tart shells onto the prepared pan, and prick the base of each square several times with a fork. Line the bottom of each tart shell with foil, and place some dried beans or rice on top of the foil to prevent the dough from rising while baking. Bake for about 15 minutes, until just a pale brown. Transfer to a wire rack and let cool.

While the pastry is cooling, prepare the filling. Place the beans, lemon juice and zest, olive oil, oregano, and fennel in a food processor, and process until smooth. Season to taste with salt and pepper. Divide the filling among the tart shells. Place the cherry tomatoes randomly over the top of the filling. Bake for 10 to 12 minutes, until the bean mixture is heated through and tomatoes are just starting to soften.

Serve hot or at room temperature, with a drizzle of balsamic vinegar and a squeeze of lemon.

MAKES 4 TO 6 TARTS

Pine Nut Pastry

1/2 cup pine nuts

1 1/2 cups flour

2 tablespoons extra virgin olive oil or hazelnut oil

1/2 cup very cold skim milk

Filling

1 cup cooked or canned, drained cannellini beans

1 tablespoon freshly squeezed lemon juice

1 teaspoon grated lemon zest

1 tablespoon extra virgin olive oil

Leaves from 1 sprig oregano

1 tablespoon chopped fresh fennel bulb

Pinch of salt

Freshly ground black pepper

1 cup cherry tomatoes, stemmed and halved

Balsamic vinegar, as accompaniment

Freshly squeezed lemon juice, as accompaniment

CLASSIC: SAUVIGNON BLANC
ADVENTUROUS: SANGIOVESE

Pasta, Pizza, and Rice

Cucina Garden Pizza, page 55

Linguini with Broccoli, Olives, and Walnut Sauce

SERVES 4

Walnut Sauce

1/2 cup walnut halves, blanched

1/3 cup fresh breadcrumbs

2 tablespoons ricotta cheese

Juice and grated zest of 1/2 lemon

1 teaspoon fresh rosemary leaves

1/2 teaspoon crushed garlic

1 tablespoon freshly grated Parmesan cheese

Salt and freshly ground black pepper

14 ounces dried linguini

1/4 cup dry white wine

2 cups broccoli florets

1/4 cup chopped black olives

4 to 6 leaves fresh basil, torn into small pieces

The flavors of broccoli and walnuts go together wonderfully, especially in this rich, creamy sauce that comes together very quickly. You could substitute any of your favorite vegetables or even add cooked chicken or prawns.

To make the walnut sauce, bring a saucepan of water to a boil over high heat. Add the walnuts and blanch for 1 minute, then drain. Place the walnuts in a food processor with the breadcrumbs, ricotta, lemon juice and zest, rosemary, garlic, and Parmesan, and process to a coarse paste, adding a little water if it is too thick. Season to taste with salt and pepper; set aside.

To prepare the pasta and finish the dish, cook the linguini according to the package directions. When the pasta is nearly cooked, bring the wine to a boil in a small saucepan over high heat. Add the broccoli, cover the pan with a lid, and cook just until crisp-tender, 2 to 3 minutes. Add the olives and basil and cook, uncovered, just until the basil is wilted. When the pasta is cooked, drain well and place it in a large bowl. Add the broccoli mixture and cooking liquid, and toss well. Serve immediately in shallow bowls, topped with the walnut sauce.

CLASSIC: CHARDONNAY

ADVENTUROUS: OLDER SPARKLING BLANC DE NOIRS OR ROSÉ

Angel Hair Pasta with Clams, White Wine, and Prosciutto Crumble

One of my favorite ways to come up with a new recipe is to get ideas or inspiration from friends, which become concepts for me to take home and experiment with. The essence of this recipe was inspired by a favorite dish of a wonderful man and great friend, the general manager of Villagio and Vintage Inn, David Shipman. David suggested the added flavor and crunch of a prosciutto crumble for this classic Italian pasta dish. Visually this dish is more stunning when served with the clams in the shell, but less fussy if you remove them—the choice is yours.

To make the crumble, heat 1 teaspoon of the olive oil in a nonstick sauté pan until hot. Add the prosciutto and sauté until the meat starts to crisp, about 1 to 2 minutes. Add the breadcrumbs and continue cooking, stirring often, until the mixture is browned and crispy, about 2 minutes longer. Remove the pan from the heat. Add the remaining 1 teaspoon of olive oil and the lemon zest and juice and basil. Mix well with a fork to form a crumble; set aside.

To prepare the pasta, cook it according to the package directions, drain well, leave it in the colander, and toss with a little olive oil; set aside.

While the pasta is cooking, place the wine, garlic, and thyme in a large, heavy saucepan over high heat, and bring to a boil. Add the clams, cover with a lid, and cook until the clams have opened, about 5 minutes. Remove each clam from the pan as it opens and transfer to a bowl, tipping all the liquid back into the pan. Give a tap with a knife to any that do not open and cook 1 to 2 minutes longer; if they still do not open, discard. Continue to cook the wine mixture over medium to high heat for 5 to 10 minutes to concentrate the flavors.

To finish the dish, add the pasta and the clams to the pan and reheat gently over low heat. Add the tomatoes and parsley, and toss well. Serve immediately in large, shallow bowls, with the crumble scattered over the top.

CLASSIC: SAUVIGNON BLANC/PINOT GRIGIO

ADVENTUROUS: SANGIOVESE

SERVES 4

Prosciutto Crumble

2 teaspoons extra virgin olive oil

2 thin slices lean prosciutto, such as Hobbs, finely diced

1/4 cup fresh coarse breadcrumbs

2 teaspoons freshly grated lemon zest

1 tablespoon freshly squeezed lemon juice

1 tablespoon chopped fresh basil

Pasta

8 to 10 ounces dried angel hair pasta or spaghettini

2 cups white wine, such as a fruity or grassy Sauvignon Blanc, a Chardonnay, or a Riesling

2 to 3 cloves garlic, chopped

1 sprig thyme

16 to 20 medium clams, rinsed well

3 to 4 finely diced medium vine-ripened tomatoes

1/2 cup chopped fresh parsley

Pasta with Zinfandel Prawns, Watercress, and Mint-Tarragon Oil

Zinfandel is a wonderful red wine grape grown in abundance around Yountville. For this recipe, the prawns are cooked in the wine along with ingredients that accentuate its complex flavors. The watercress brings out the Zinfandel's peppery notes, while the slightly anise tone of the tarragon matches the Zinfandel's cassis aroma. Scallops also work well with this dish, as their plump, moist texture soaks up the wine nicely.

To make the mint-tarragon oil, bring a small saucepan of water to a boil over high heat, add the herbs, and blanch for 1 minute. Drain immediately, then plunge in a bowl of ice water to shock, or stop the cooking process. Drain well, then use paper towels to squeeze out as much moisture as possible. Place the herbs in a food processor with the olive oil, and process until smooth; set aside.

To prepare the pasta, cook it according to the package directions, drain well, and place in a large bowl. Toss with 1 tablespoon of the olive oil; set aside.

To prepare the prawns, heat the remaining 1 tablespoon of olive oil in a large pan until hot. Add the onion and sauté for 1 minute. Add the prawns and sauté until just cooked, 1 to 2 minutes. Transfer to a plate; set aside.

To finish the dish, pour the wine into the pan and reduce over medium heat until it is thick and resembles a light syrup, about 10 minutes. Return the prawn mixture to the pan, and stir well. Add the watercress and pasta, toss well to coat the pasta with the sauce, and cook just until heated through.

Serve immediately in shallow bowls, drizzled with the herb oil and garnished with a sprinkle of Parmesan.

CLASSIC: NAPA VALLEY ZINFANDEL
ADVENTUROUS: GEWÜRZTRAMINER

SERVES 4

Mint-Tarragon Oil

1/2 cup fresh mint leaves
1/4 cup fresh tarragon leaves
1/2 cup extra virgin olive oil

1 package (12 ounces) dried campanelle, farfalle, or other short pasta
2 tablespoons extra virgin olive oil
1/4 cup finely diced red onion or fennel
20 large uncooked prawns, shelled and deveined
3/4 cup Zinfandel
1 cup fresh watercress leaves
Freshly grated Parmesan cheese, for garnish

Stir-Fried Scallops and Grapes with Spaghetti

SERVES 4

1 package (14 ounces) dried
    spaghetti noodles

2 tablespoons extra virgin olive oil

2 green onions, white and green
    parts, chopped

1 tablespoon peeled, chopped
    fresh ginger

1 red bell pepper, stemmed,
    seeded, ribbed, and diced

16 to 20 large scallops

1 cup green seedless grapes

2 tablespoons chopped fresh
    Italian parsley

1/2 cup dry white wine

2 tablespoons chopped fresh
    chives, for garnish

So often, we limit the use of grapes to snacking on, but they are great when heated until they are just about to burst, and tossed into a main dish such as this one. Here, I've used scallops as the focus of the recipe, but prawns, salmon, or swordfish taste just as delicious.

Cook the pasta according to the package directions. Drain and toss with 1 tablespoon of the olive oil. Keep warm in a colander set over a pan of water on low heat.

Heat the remaining 1 tablespoon of olive oil in a large, nonstick sauté pan or wok over high heat until hot. Add the onions, ginger, and bell pepper, and stir-fry until just tender, 1 to 2 minutes. Add the scallops and stir-fry until just cooked through, but still plump and tender, 1 to 2 minutes. Add the grapes, parsley, and wine, cover with a lid, decrease the heat to medium, and cook just long enough to heat all the ingredients through, about 30 seconds to 1 minute. Add the reserved spaghetti and toss well. Serve immediately, garnished with the chives.

CLASSIC: MATURE CHARDONNAY
ADVENTUROUS: DRY RIESLING

Cucina Garden Pizza

Colorful tomatoes in season, moist fresh mozzarella, fruity olive oil, and tender basil leaves are classic Italian partners and often tagged "Caprese." This combination forms the basis of one of Cucina's most popular and delectable, yet simple, pizzas, and no wonder, as you almost feel you're in Italy while enjoying pizza amid the bright yellow umbrellas, overhanging vines, and cobblestone wall backdrop. Create your own Italian atmosphere to get the most out of experiencing this pizza—a red checkered tablecloth, Italian opera, and, of course, a simple Italian red.

To make the pizza dough, combine the flours, salt, yeast, and sugar in the bowl of an electric mixer fitted with the dough hook (or a large mixing bowl if mixing by hand). Combine the honey, olive oil, and 1 cup of the water in a medium bowl, and pour it into the dry ingredients. Mix on low speed, adding as much of the remaining water as needed to form a smooth, firm, and elastic dough.

Remove the dough from the mixing bowl. Turn the dough out onto a lightly floured board and knead briefly to form it into a ball, place it in a large bowl, and cover with a damp towel. Let rise in a warm place for 15 to 20 minutes. Punch the dough down, divide it into 6 to 8 pieces, and form each piece into a smooth ball. Place the dough in a sealed plastic container and let rise in the refrigerator for at least 15 to 20 minutes. (You can keep the dough in the refrigerator, properly sealed, for up to three days).

To assemble the pizzas, if using a pizza stone, set it in the oven. Preheat the oven to 425°F. Press or roll out each ball of dough into a circle about 1/8 inch thick. If using a pizza stone, place the dough on a well-floured pizza peel; or place it on a well-oiled baking sheet. Top with tomato and mozzarella slices. Gently slide the pizza onto the hot pizza stone, or set the baking sheet in the oven. Bake the pizza for 7 to 10 minutes, until the crust is golden brown and crisp (the pizza will cook more quickly on a pizza stone than a baking sheet, so keep an eye on it). Remove the pizza from the oven, drizzle with some of the basil oil, sprinkle with chopped basil, and season to taste with salt and pepper. To serve, pile a small handful of mixed greens and flowers in the center of the pizza, and serve piping hot. Continue preparing pizzas or store the remaining dough in the refrigerator or freezer for future use.

CLASSIC: SAUVIGNON BLANC OR SANGIOVESE (100%)
ADVENTUROUS: BONE-DRY SPARKLING BLANC DE BLANCS

STEFAN RICHTER WITH SOUS CHEF JOSH WHITE VILLAGIO INN & SPA AND CUCINA À LA CARTE

MAKES 6 TO 9 INDIVIDUAL PIZZAS

Pizza Dough

3 1/2 cups all-purpose flour
1/4 cup whole-wheat flour
2 teaspoons salt
1 1/2 tablespoons active dry yeast
1 teaspoon sugar
1 tablespoon honey
2 tablespoons olive oil
1 1/2 to 2 cups warm water

Topping

Thinly sliced ripe seasonal tomatoes
Thinly sliced fresh mozzarella
Basil Oil (page 42)
Fresh basil leaves, chopped
Freshly ground salt and pepper
Mixed baby greens and edible flowers, for garnish

Winter Squash and Basil Risotto with Parmesan-Macadamia Shards

SERVES 4

Parmesan-Macadamia Shards

1/2 cup freshly shredded Parmesan cheese

2 tablespoons finely diced macadamia nuts

1 teaspoon freshly grated lemon zest

Extra virgin olive oil

2 tablespoons extra virgin olive oil

1 clove garlic, crushed

1 onion, chopped

1 1/2 cups arborio rice

1 cup dry white or sparkling wine

2 cups diced winter squash, such as butternut

4 cups chicken stock (page 23), kept at a simmer

1/2 cup fresh basil leaves, torn into small pieces

Juice and grated zest of 1/2 orange

Freshly cracked black pepper

With its delicate sweetness and smooth texture, winter squash makes a perfect companion to a rich, creamy risotto. Try preparing this dish with some of the abundant squash that starts appearing around Halloween. The Parmesan-Macadamia Shards add a pleasing contrast of texture to the risotto, as well as a fabulous macadamia flavor that pairs nicely with the sweetness of the squash.

To make the shards, preheat the broiler. In a small bowl, combine the Parmesan, nuts, and zest. Heat a large ovenproof nonstick sauté pan over medium-high heat and brush with a bit of the olive oil. Place tablespoonfuls of the mixture at least 1 inch apart in the pan and press with a wooden spoon to evenly flatten. Cook until the cheese is just melted, then set the pan under the broiler and broil for 20 to 30 minutes, until golden brown. Remove the shards carefully with a spatula, place on a wire rack, and let cool completely.

To prepare the risotto, heat the olive oil in a large, heavy saucepan over medium heat until hot. Add the garlic and onion, and sauté until translucent, 1 to 2 minutes. Add the rice and sauté until all the grains are well coated with oil, 1 to 2 minutes. Add the wine and cook, stirring continuously, until all the liquid is absorbed. Fold in the squash, then add the chicken stock, a ladle at a time, stirring often and allowing the liquid to absorb before each addition. When all the liquid is absorbed and the rice is tender and creamy, about 20 minutes, add the basil and the orange juice and zest, mix well, and season to taste with pepper. Cover the pan with a lid, remove from the heat, and let sit for 5 minutes before serving.

Serve warm, in large, shallow bowls, garnished with the shards.

CLASSIC: PINOT BLANC
ADVENTUROUS: MERLOT

SERVES 4

Sushi Rice

2 cups medium- or short-grain
    sushi rice (or white rice)

2 1/4 cups cold water

6 tablespoons rice vinegar

3 tablespoons sugar

1/2 teaspoon salt

Salad

1/2 pound cooked bay shrimp

3 tablespoons seasoned rice
    vinegar

1 teaspoon peeled, minced fresh
    ginger

1 carrot, peeled and julienned

1 teaspoon Chinese red chile oil

1 cup freshly shelled peas

1 tablespoon toasted sesame oil

Tahini Sauce

1/4 cup mayonnaise

1/4 cup tahini

1 tablespoon mirin

1 tablespoon seasoned rice vinegar

1 tablespoon freshly squeezed
    lime juice

1 tablespoon peeled, grated fresh
    ginger

2 teaspoons sesame oil

Sushi Salad with Nori-Wrapped Tempura Ahi

Here is a delicious illustration of Kinyon Gordon's skills in combining both simple and slightly exotic flavors in a dish that wows, but that is also totally accessible to the home cook. You'll find wasabi, along with mirin, sesame oil, and nori—which is toasted seaweed—in the Asian section of most supermarkets. For this recipe, Kinyon uses two different sesame oils—a dark, toasted one for the salad and regular sesame oil to add just a hint of flavor to the sauce.

To prepare the sushi rice, place the rice in a strainer and rinse under cold water until the water runs clear. Drain well. Transfer the rice to a heavy medium saucepan. Add the water and bring the mixture to a boil over high heat. Decrease the heat to low, cover with a tight-fitting lid, and cook for 15 minutes, until the water is absorbed and the rice is just tender. Resist the urge to lift the lid during cooking, as you don't want the steam to escape. Remove the pan from the heat and let stand, covered, for 15 minutes. Transfer the rice to a large bowl; set aside.

Combine the vinegar, sugar, and salt in a small saucepan over low heat, and cook, stirring continuously, until the sugar dissolves. Drizzle the vinegar mixture over the rice and gently toss to coat. Cover with a clean, damp towel and let cool completely. Do not refrigerate.

To make the salad, in three separate bowls, toss the shrimp with the vinegar and ginger; toss the carrots with the chile oil; and toss the peas with the sesame oil. Place the bowls in the refrigerator to marinate.

To make the tahini sauce, place all the ingredients in a food processor or blender and process until smooth. Transfer the sauce to a bowl, cover with plastic wrap, and refrigerate until ready to use.

Just before serving, prepare the tempura. In large bowl, beat the egg then whisk in the club soda. Add the 1 cup flour and whisk just until smooth (it's okay if the batter is slightly lumpy). Lay a half sheet of nori on a clean, dry work surface and spread with 1 teaspoon of the wasabi. Place a strip of ahi across the end of one of the short sides of the nori, and roll up to form a cigar shape. Repeat with the remaining nori and ahi.

Heat 2 inches of peanut oil in a large, heavy saucepan over high heat until it reaches 350°F. Place the 1/4 cup flour on a plate. Lightly dredge each ahi roll in the flour, then dip in the batter and carefully place in the hot oil. Deep-fry until golden brown and just crisp, 30 to 45 seconds. Transfer to paper towels to drain, then cut in half diagonally.

To assemble the salad, place a generous spoonful of the sushi rice in each of 4 deep bowls. Divide the carrots, peas, and shrimp among the bowls, placing each in a mound over the rice. Sprinkle with the green onions. Place 2 halves of the freshly cooked ahi, cut side up, in the center of the rice. Drizzle lightly with tahini sauce and sprinkle with toasted sesame seeds. Serve immediately.

Note: To toast the sesame seeds, place them in a skillet over medium-high heat. Toss them continuously in the skillet until they begin to turn a light golden color. Transfer the sesame seeds to a plate and spread them out in a single layer to cool.

CLASSIC: SAUVIGNON BLANC OR PINOT GRIS
ADVENTUROUS: CALIFORNIA RED RHONE BLEND
(MIXTURE OF GRENACHE, SYRAH, AND MOUVEDRE)

Nori-Wrapped Tempura Ahi

1 egg

1 cup ice-cold club soda

1 cup plus $1/4$ cup flour

2 nori sheets, halved

4 teaspoons wasabi paste, or to taste

12 ounces ahi tuna fillet, cut into 4 long strips

Peanut or olive oil for deep frying

$1/2$ cup chopped green onion, white and green parts, for garnish

1 tablespoon toasted sesame seeds, for garnish (see note)

KINYON GORDON, KINYON CAFÉ AND CATERING

Kinyon has become a household name in Yountville and its surrounds, for his infectious charm and radiance and, of course, his café's consistently great food. He is the caterer that everyone wants to have as a dinner guest. He is Café Kinyon, where "lunchers" sit in eager anticipation, hoping he'll come beaming through his office door to greet them.

In Yountville, where his business has thrived for over twelve years, Kinyon has found what is a common thread in this "small town of many chefs"—a life he loves. He deals directly with local food producers and is constantly challenged to meet the sometimes very obscure demands of his clients. All this adds up, not to work for Kinyon, but to a great life.

Kinyon's food is so varied that it's hard to put a label on it. In his café, he creates dishes that are simple, yet have a spark of life and fun. His catering menu ranges from visually stunning creations to multicultural feasts or bountiful comfort food. He is a man with no fear of food who loves to be put to the test.

Kinyon's ultimate day of relaxation is to have an intense morning workout, then walk to a local café for coffee and a newspaper. He'll then come home and float in the pool for awhile, have a snooze, and maybe float some more. The day is capped off with a spontaneous dinner party for friends. He is, in a word, content.

Wild Rice and Farro Salad

Farro is the whole grain of the wheat and is commonly used in Italian cooking. Its earthy flavor and crunchy texture make a great match with the wild rice in this recipe, but if you can't find it, use wheat berries instead. Try this dish warm or cold, as an accompaniment to your favorite vegetables or grilled meats.

SERVES 4 TO 6

3/4 cup wild rice

3/4 cup farro or whole wheat berries

1 (2-inch-long) piece ginger, peeled and thinly sliced

6 to 8 large mushrooms, such as a mix of shiitake and white, sliced

6 dried apricot halves, sliced

1 small red onion, halved and thinly sliced

6 spears asparagus, ends trimmed and sliced thinly on the diagonal

1/2 bunch cilantro, coarsely chopped

Grated zest and juice of 1 lemon

2 to 3 tablespoons extra virgin olive oil

A few drops truffle oil (optional)

Toasted slivered almonds, for garnish (see note)

Place the rice and farro in a large pot of cold salted water. Bring to a boil over high heat, then decrease the heat and simmer for 10 minutes. Remove the pan from the heat, cover with a lid, and let the grains steam for 30 minutes. Return the pan to medium heat and simmer, loosely covered, until tender, 10 to 15 minutes longer. Drain and rinse well with cold water.

While the grains are cooking, place the ginger, mushrooms, apricots, and a few tablespoons of water in a small saucepan over medium heat and steam, uncovered, just until tender, 2 to 3 minutes. Remove the pan from the heat. Let mixture sit in the pan for 5 to 10 minutes so the flavors infuse into the water.

Transfer the grains to a large bowl. Add the mushroom mixture, onions, asparagus, cilantro, and lemon zest, and toss. In a small bowl, combine the lemon juice, olive oil, and truffle oil, add it to the salad, and toss well. Serve warm or cold, garnished with slivered almonds.

Note: To toast the almonds, place them in a skillet over medium-high heat. Toss them continuously in the skillet until they begin to turn a light golden color. Transfer the almonds to a plate and spread them out in a single layer to cool.

CLASSIC: DRY CALIFORNIA ROSÉ
ADVENTUROUS: MERLOT

Fish and Seafood

Opaka-Paka with Chestnut Butter and White Asparagus, page 64

ERIC TORRALBA
DOMAINE CHANDON

C

SERVES 4

2 tablespoons extra virgin olive oil

1 eggplant, peeled and diced into
    $1/2$-inch cubes

1 teaspoon unsalted butter

1 small pumpkin, peeled and diced
    into $1/2$-inch cubes

12 spears white asparagus, trimmed

1 egg (see note)

Salt and freshly ground black pepper

5 fresh chestnuts, ground in a food
    processor to a fine powder

Sauce

$1/2$ bottle of Chandon Brut Reserve

1 shallot, peeled and diced

Reserved chestnut powder

2 tablespoons heavy whipping
    cream

2 tablespoons unsalted butter

Salt and freshly ground black pep-
    per

Extra virgin olive oil for cooking

4 (7-ounce) opaka-paka fillets, or
    mahi-mahi, opah, or other firm-
    fleshed white fish

Chervil, for garnish

Note: If you have doubts about
using raw eggs, you can substitute a
pasteurized egg product instead.

Opaka-Paka with Chestnut Butter and White Asparagus

When I met Eric Torralba, I instantly discovered his unfettered passion for the dishes he prepares and his manner of bringing whatever the garden offers to the plate. This simply prepared dish is stunning to behold and fits right into the exquisite surroundings of Domaine Chandon, and it will be equally stunning on your dinner table. Both the opaka-paka and white asparagus have delicate flavors and textures, perfect for pairing with fresh vegetables of your choice.

To prepare the vegetables, heat 1 tablespoon of the olive oil in a medium sauté pan over medium-high heat until hot. Add the eggplant and sauté until soft, 3 to 5 minutes. Drain the excess liquid and transfer the eggplant to a plate; set aside. Add the remaining tablespoon of olive oil and the butter to the pan, and heat over medium-high heat until the butter melts. Add the pumpkin and sauté until soft, 2 to 3 minutes; set aside.

Bring a large pan of salted water to a boil over high heat. Add the asparagus and blanch until tender, about 6 minutes. Drain, rinse under cold water, and pat dry. In a small bowl, lightly beat the egg with salt and pepper. Place the chestnut powder on a small plate. Dip the top of each asparagus spear in the egg then dust with the chestnut powder (reserve the remaining chestnut powder for the sauce). Place the asparagus on a plate, and cover with plastic wrap until ready to serve.

To prepare the sauce, combine the Chandon Brut Reserve with the shallot and the remaining chestnut powder in a medium saucepan over high heat. Bring to a boil, then decrease the heat and simmer until reduced by about two-thirds. Slowly stir in the cream. Transfer the mixture to a blender, add the butter, and blend until smooth. Season to taste with salt and pepper. Pour the sauce back into the pan, cover with a lid, and keep warm.

To prepare the fish, heat enough olive oil to coat the base of a sauté pan over medium heat until hot. Add the fillets, skin side down, and sauté for 3 to 4 minutes, or until the fish is white and opaque or just starts to flake when tested with a fork.

On individual plates, arrange the asparagus spears over the vegetables, then top with a warm opaka-paka fillet. Brush the fish with olive oil, spoon some of the sauce around the vegetables, and garnish with chervil, melissa, or other fresh herbs. Enjoy and stay healthy!

WINE PAIRING BY DAVID BRIDGES, WINE CAPTAIN, DOMAINE CHANDON
CLASSIC: CHANDON CHARDONNAY, WITH ITS FRESH CHARACTER
AND DRY FINISH WITH MORE BODY.
ADVENTUROUS: THE CHANDON ÉTOILE IS A CITRUSY, FRESH AND CRISP SPARKLING
WINE THAT WOULD COMPLEMENT THE DISH BEAUTIFULLY.

ERIC TORRALBA, DOMAINE CHANDON RESTAURANT

Arriving at Domaine Chandon from the south of France, Eric Torralba was resolved to bring all he believed and knew to his new location. He is an energetic, charming man who has a spark of rebellion and determination and has brought this essence to Chandon.

Eric doesn't follow trends or go by recipes. He starts with the ingredients and works with them, weaving them intricately into the style of dishes he has come to be known for. His food ends like a designer "splash" on a plate, intentionally balanced and yet random, the flavors focused and yet playful.

One part of Eric loves to experiment with different ingredients such as sunchokes or Pecorino, yet he also thrives on taking everyday inexpensive items and turning them into something stunning. To this end he will explore boundaries and pick unusual plants to grow such as vanilla and saffron, though he also supports the local farmers. Eric believes diners come to Domaine Chandon to have a good time and eat exceptional food, and that each bite should speak for itself.

His personal therapy is to drink sage tea or thyme tea if he is feeling off balance. But he's always ready to pour you a glass of Domaine Chandon's sparkling wines. Relaxation for Eric means a long drive with nice music, and he loves that in the valley he isn't bombarded with billboards and advertising. A true Frenchman, he has raised his daughter to enjoy a sip of good wine as well as tea, a practice he assures, with a wink, that is why French children are so well behaved in restaurants.

Slow-Roasted Salmon with Wilted Spinach and Truffle Mashed Potatoes

SERVES 4

4 (6-ounce) salmon fillets, skin and bones removed
2 tablespoons extra virgin olive oil
Sea salt
Freshly ground black pepper
2 tablespoons fresh oregano leaves
1 sprig rosemary

Truffle Mashed Potatoes

4 medium white potatoes, peeled and diced
$1/4$ cup buttermilk or milk
1 tablespoon extra virgin olive oil
$1/2$ teaspoon truffle oil, or to taste
Salt and freshly ground black pepper

4 handfuls baby spinach leaves
Lemon wedges, for garnish

Most people recommend cooking fish quickly at high heat for the best results, but this slow-roasting method is terrific for fish such as salmon and sea trout or even octopus. At the end of the cooking time, the fish may still appear uncooked, as it doesn't change color, but I guarantee that it will just melt in your mouth. Add a creamy bed of truffle mashed potatoes and some wilted spinach, and you've got an elegant, yet comforting, dish.

To prepare the salmon, preheat the oven to 200°F. Place the salmon fillets, side-by-side and in a single layer, in a casserole dish. Drizzle with the olive oil, season with salt and pepper to taste, and sprinkle with the oregano. Lay the sprig of rosemary over the fillets. Bake for 25 to 30 minutes, until the fish just flakes when pressed with a fork.

While the fish is cooking, prepare the mashed potatoes. Place the potatoes in a large saucepan, add enough cold water to cover, and bring to a boil over high heat. Lower the heat and simmer until tender. Drain well. Add the buttermilk, olive oil, and truffle oil, and mash until smooth. Season to taste with salt and pepper. Cover with a lid to keep warm until ready to serve.

To prepare the spinach, bring about $1/4$ cup of water to a boil in a saucepan over medium heat. Add the spinach, cover with a lid, and simmer for 30 to 40 seconds, just until wilted. Drain and cover with a lid to keep warm.

When fish is done, divide the mashed potatoes among individual plates and top with the salmon. Serve immediately, with lemon wedges for garnish and the spinach on the side.

CLASSIC: CHARDONNAY
ADVENTUROUS: PINOT NOIR

Grilled Swordfish with Warm Corn and Bean Salad

Swordfish is very popular in the Mediterranean, especially southern Italy, where it is one of the staples and usually simply prepared grilled with lemon and oil. Serving this salad alongside is one of my favorite ways to add a splash of color, flavor, and texture, and still keep it a quick and healthy meal—even quicker than ordering out for pizza!

To prepare the salad, combine the vinegar, lime juice, and 2 teaspoons of the olive oil in a jar, and shake well; set aside. Heat the remaining 2 teaspoons of olive oil in a nonstick sauté pan or wok over medium-high heat until hot. Add the corn, onions, and bell peppers, and sauté just until tender, 3 to 4 minutes. Add the beans and toss well. Cook until the beans are just heated through, about 1 to 2 minutes. Cover with a lid and keep warm.

To prepare the swordfish, preheat a grill pan or nonstick pan to high heat. Brush the steaks with olive oil and grill for 2 to 3 minutes per side, until just tender and still moist in the center or to preferred doneness

To serve, divide the corn salad among individual plates and garnish with cilantro. Top with the swordfish steaks and drizzle with the dressing. Serve immediately.

CLASSIC: VIOGNIER
ADVENTUROUS: PINOT NOIR

SERVES 4

Warm Corn and Bean Salad

- 1 tablespoon raspberry or red wine vinegar
- 2 tablespoon freshly squeezed lime juice
- 4 teaspoons extra virgin olive oil
- Freshly cut kernels from 2 large ears corn
- 2 green onions, white and green parts, chopped
- 1/2 red bell pepper, stemmed, seeded, ribbed, and diced
- 1/2 cup cannellini beans, cooked and rinsed

- 4 (6-ounce) swordfish steaks
- Extra virgin olive oil, for brushing
- 1/4 cup chopped fresh cilantro, for garnish

Olive Oil-Poached Swordfish with Sweet Pepper Stew

JEFF CERCIELLO
BOUCHON

This is an unusual method for cooking fish (but one commonly used in France), and it produces a very tender and surprisingly light fillet of fish. Slow cooking in extra virgin olive oil tenderizes the fish and brings a rich and mildly fruity flavor. Make sure you use a quality extra virgin olive oil for the best result. Jeff has paired the swordfish perfectly with a sweet pepper stew that not only complements the fish but also makes a beautiful color contrast. He recommends preparing the stew a day or two ahead of time for the flavors to fully develop (and to save you preparation time the day you serve the dish).

To prepare the stew, preheat the oven to 450°F, with the rack set in the middle. Line two baking sheets with aluminum foil.

In a large bowl, toss the red and yellow peppers with the olive oil and 1 teaspoon kosher salt. Place the red peppers, cut side down and in a single layer, on one of the prepared pans; place the yellow peppers on the other pan. Roast the peppers for 15 to 20 minutes, until the skin has blistered and browned. (The yellow peppers will probably roast more quickly, so keep an eye on them.) Transfer the peppers to a bowl, cover with plastic wrap, and let sit for about 10 minutes to steam and cool.

When the roasted peppers are cool enough to handle, peel off and discard the skins, working over a bowl to catch any juices. Cut the peppers into 1/2-inch strips, then cut crosswise into 1/2-inch dice. Combine the roasted peppers and their juices with the piquillo peppers and the 1/2 cup chicken stock in a saucepan over medium heat, and season to taste with salt and pepper. Add the vinegar and simmer until the liquid is slightly reduced and the flavors have melded, 8 to 10 minutes. Remove the pan from the heat and keep warm; or, if you've prepared the stew in advance, cover and refrigerate until ready to use. (The stew may be made up to 3 days in advance.)

To prepare the swordfish, place the fillets in a single layer in a high-sided pan or saucepan just large enough for the fillets to fit snugly. Add enough olive oil to cover the fish by 1/2 inch. Lift the fish from the oil and place on a plate. Place the sprigs of thyme and head of garlic in the oil. Place the pan over low heat and warm the oil until it reaches 140°F. Remove the pan from the heat. Place the fillets in the oil, thyme, and garlic and let sit to cook until opaque, about 10 to 12 minutes. The temperature of the oil will decrease, so watch the thermometer and set the pan back on the stove as needed to keep the oil between

SERVES 4

Sweet Pepper Stew

4 large red bell peppers, halved, stemmed, seeded, and ribbed

4 large yellow bell peppers, halved, stemmed, seeded, and ribbed

1/4 cup extra virgin olive oil

Kosher salt

1/2 cup piquillo peppers, seeded and diced

1/2 cup plus 1/4 cup chicken stock (page 23)

Freshly ground black pepper

Dash of red wine vinegar

4 (6-ounce) swordfish fillets, 1 to 1/2 inch thick, skinned

Extra virgin olive oil, for cooking

4 sprigs thyme

1 small head of garlic, halved, horizontally

Fleur de sel (sea salt)

Freshly ground black pepper

4 teaspoons minced fresh parsley, for garnish

125°F and 140°F. The fish can be kept warm in the oil for several minutes while you finish preparing the dish.

To finish the dish, place the stew in a saucepan over medium heat, adding the 1/4 cup chicken stock. Simmer to heat the peppers and reduce the liquid slightly, 1 to 2 minutes.

To serve, divide the stew between 4 serving plates. Using a spatula, carefully remove the fillets from the oil, blot with a paper towel, and place over the stew. Sprinkle with fleur de sel and pepper to taste, and drizzle with a little olive oil. Garnish with parsley, and serve immediately.

CLASSIC: CHARDONNAY OR AGED SPARKLING BRUT
ADVENTUROUS: DOLCETTO

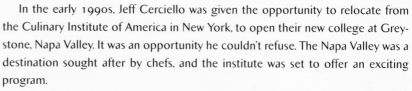

JEFF CERCIELLO, BOUCHON

In the early 1990s, Jeff Cerciello was given the opportunity to relocate from the Culinary Institute of America in New York, to open their new college at Greystone, Napa Valley. It was an opportunity he couldn't refuse. The Napa Valley was a destination sought after by chefs, and the institute was set to offer an exciting program.

The multicultural focus of Greystone's CIA suited Jeff perfectly, as he had traveled and cooked extensively in Spain and other European destinations. Over time, Jeff realized that if he were to come back to the States, the Napa Valley was the only place that could mimic the aspect of Europe he had so come to love—the combination of food, wine, terrain, and food professionals. To Jeff, it was the cutting edge.

Returning to a position at The French Laundry only further confirmed that he had made the right decision. Jeff recalls that working with Thomas Keller opened his eyes to a whole new world of food, a total experience from the daily changing menu and the attention to finesse and detail, to the ultimate hunt for suppliers that could guarantee the highest quality produce. When Thomas decided to open Bouchon, Jeff jumped at the challenge.

Now heading the kitchens, Jeff thrives on the challenge of meeting the expectations of the clientele who dine at Bouchon. Their palates are discerning and their expectations high. Jeff's goal is to make each experience better than the last.

Relaxation for Jeff means to go fly-fishing and to take his wife and young daughter on picnics. To destress, Jeff enjoys a 25-mile bike ride followed by a soak in a hot tub, and he firmly believes in never taking work home—that's time out.

Grouper en Papillote with Lemon Verbena Rice

RYAN JACKSON, BRIX

Ryan Jackson created this recipe with aromatic lemon verbena leaves as the flavor basis. The expansive garden at Brix abounds with fresh herbs and vegetables—perfect for inspiring delectable new creations. Cooking fish "en papillote" is a classic French style of steaming fish and gives moist and tender results, capturing all of the aromas and flavors in one parcel.

To prepare the rice, place the verbena leaves and canola oil in a small saucepan over medium heat, and bring to a light simmer. Remove the pan from the heat and let stand for 30 minutes. Strain the oil through a fine-mesh sieve into a small bowl, discarding the verbena; set aside. If not using immediately, let cool, cover with plastic wrap, and refrigerate. The oil will keep for up to 2 weeks. Cook the basmati and wild rice according to the package directions. Cover and keep warm until ready to serve. Just before serving, combine the basmati and wild rice in a serving bowl and toss with a little of the verbena oil.

While the rice is cooking, prepare the fish. Preheat the oven to 375°F. Fold four 14- to 16-inch-long sheets of parchment paper in half. Cut each into half-moon shapes, the length of the sheet, so when the paper is opened it is in a heart shape.

Place 1 sheet of parchment paper on a flat work surface and brush both sides of the fold with olive oil. Sprinkle salt, pepper, and one-fourth of the shallots over the center of one half of the paper. Place a fillet over the seasoning, and sprinkle one-fourth of the peppers, celery, shallots, chipotles, lemon and lime zest, and coconut over the top. Drizzle with about 2 tablespoons of the wine and finish with a dab of butter. Fold over the other half of the parchment paper to match the edges of the bottom half. Fold the bottom corner in about 1/2 inch and continue folding all the way around to seal the package into a half-moon shape. Continue with the remaining parchment and ingredients. Place the parchment packages on a baking sheet, set the pan in the oven, and bake for 10 minutes, until the fish is tender (the parchment should be brown and puffed up).

To serve, place the unopened packages on individual plates, so you can open them at the table and experience the sublime escaping aromas. Serve immediately, with the warm scented rice on the side.

CLASSIC: SAUVIGNON BLANC
ADVENTUROUS: VIOGNIER

SERVES 4

Lemon Verbena Rice

3 leaves lemon verbena
1/2 cup canola oil
2 cups basmati rice
1 cup wild rice

Grouper

Parchment paper
Olive oil, for brushing
Salt and freshly ground black pepper
1 shallot, diced, for prepping the parchment
4 fillets (about 1 1/2 pounds each) New Zealand grouper, halibut, snapper, sturgeon, or other firm white fish fillets
1 red bell pepper, stemmed, seeded, ribbed, and sliced into thin strips
1 yellow bell pepper, stemmed, seeded, ribbed, and sliced into thin strips
3 ribs celery, thinly sliced
2 shallots, diced
2 dried chipotle chiles, soaked in boiling water for 5 to 10 minutes, then stemmed, seeded, and chopped
1 tablespoon freshly grated lemon zest
1 tablespoon freshly grated lime zest
1/4 cup flaked coconut
1/2 cup dry white wine
4 teaspoons butter

SERVES 4

2 large or 4 small whole river trout (about 12 to 14 ounces each), boned, filleted, heads removed

Herb Mousse

1 tablespoon chopped fresh thyme

2 tablespoons chopped fresh parsley

1 tablespoon chopped fresh dill

Pinch of salt

Pinch of freshly ground black pepper

1/2 teaspoon freshly grated lemon zest

About 1/2 cup reserved trout trimmings

1/2 cup milk

1/4 cup extra virgin olive oil

Lemon-Olive Sauce

1 cup fish stock (page 23)

Juice of 1 lemon

2 tablespoons chopped shallot

Salt and freshly ground black pepper

1 tablespoon chopped fresh dill

1/2 cup olive oil

2 large Yukon gold potatoes, sliced thinly with a mandoline or vegetable peeler

Olive oil

3 tablespoons fish stock (page 23)

Pinch of sugar

8 to 10 spears fresh asparagus, trimmed and sliced diagonally into 3-inch pieces

Potato-Crusted River Trout

One of Stefan Richter's passions is to relax and unwind while fishing in a local stream. He'll then bring home the trout he catches and enjoy another passion—creating a gourmet meal for his wife, Shannon, and himself. Here he has shared one of the dishes he loves to prepare.

To prepare the trout for cooking, trim the excess flesh from the head and belly. Keep trimmings and prepared fish refrigerated until ready to use.

To make the herb mousse, combine the thyme, parsley, dill, salt, pepper, lemon zest, and reserved trout trimmings in a medium bowl, and mix well. Cover with plastic wrap and place in the freezer for 30 minutes. Meanwhile, measure out the olive oil and place in the refrigerator to chill.

While the herb mixture is freezing, prepare the sauce. In a small saucepan over high heat, bring the fish stock to a boil. Decrease the heat, add the lemon juice and shallots, and simmer until reduced by about one-fourth, 5 to 6 minutes. Add the dill, and remove the pan from the heat. Using a blender, purée the sauce. While continuing to blend, slowly add the olive oil and blend until the sauce is creamy and emulsified. Season to taste with salt and pepper. Keep warm until ready to serve. If the sauce separates, purée again just before serving.

Preheat the oven to 375°F.

To finish preparing the mousse, remove the herb mixture from the freezer and transfer it to a blender. Add the milk and purée. While blending, slowly add the chilled olive oil; the mixture should almost instantly form a mousse.

To prepare the trout, spoon mousse inside each trout cavity, taking care not to overfill. Wrap each trout with potato slices. If you have trouble making them stick, heat some olive oil in a pan and brush it over the potato slices then place them around the fish, so the fish is encased in potato. Heat a large nonstick sauté pan over medium heat until hot and add enough olive oil to just coat the surface. Add the fish and sear on one side until the potato is browned, about 1 minute, then carefully turn with a spatula to brown the other side. Transfer the fish to a baking sheet and bake for about 12 minutes, until the fish is cooked through and flakes when pressed gently with a fork.

While the fish bakes, prepare the asparagus. Heat the fish stock and sugar in a small pan over medium-high heat. Add the asparagus and cook for 1 minute, until tender-crisp. Drain and keep warm.

To serve, cut each trout in half diagonally and place on individual plates with the asparagus and sauce.

CLASSIC: SEMILLON OR PINOT NOIR
ADVENTUROUS: OFF-DRY RIESLING

THOMAS KELLER
THE FRENCH LAUNDRY

Sautéed Fillet of John Dory with Vine-Ripened Tomato "Marmelade" and Heirloom Tomato Vinaigrette

SERVES 4

Tomato Vinaigrette

4 medium heirloom red tomatoes, peeled and halved, seeds left intact (see note)
3 cups extra virgin olive oil
1 tablespoon balsamic vinegar
1 tablespoon tomato paste
Kosher salt
Freshly ground black pepper

Tomato "Marmelade"

2 cups red wine vinegar
1/4 cup granulated sugar
2 cups water
2 pounds vine-ripened red tomatoes, peeled and chopped (see note)
1 cup minced shallots
1/2 cup minced yellow onion
Kosher salt
Freshly ground black pepper

2 whole John Dory (about 3 to 4 pounds total), filleted
Kosher salt
Freshly ground white pepper
Grapeseed oil, for grilling the fish
4 parsley or chervil sprigs, for garnish

This succulent dish showcases Thomas Keller's fine and instinctive sense of combining ingredients. The complementary pairing of the tomato "marmelade" and vinaigrette with the sweet, delicate flavor of the John Dory is sublime. If your local fish market doesn't carry John Dory, ask them to order it, and to fillet it for you. You can also try this recipe with halibut, cod, or another light, white, firm fish.

To make the vinaigrette, first dry the tomatoes. Preheat the oven to 250°F. Line a small baking sheet with parchment paper and place the halved tomatoes, cut side down, on the paper. Bake the tomatoes for 2 to 3 hours, or until they have dried slightly. Place the tomatoes in a small strainer lined with a piece of cheesecloth, set the strainer over a bowl (to catch any of the liquid, or tomato water, that drains from the tomatoes), and refrigerate overnight.

The next day, remove the tomatoes from the cheesecloth and reserve the tomato water in the bowl for thinning the vinaigrette as needed. (Any extra tomato water will keep, sealed and refrigerated, for up to 1 week.) Place the tomatoes in a food processor or blender and puree. With the machine running, slowly add the olive oil and process until smooth. Add the vinegar and tomato paste, and again process until smooth. Season to taste with salt and pepper. If the vinaigrette is too thick, adjust the consistency with some of the reserved tomato water. Press the vinaigrette through a fine-mesh sieve into a bowl. The consistency should be similar to that of tomato sauce.

To make the "marmelade," combine the vinegar, sugar, and water in a small saucepan over medium-high heat, and bring to a simmer. Decrease the heat and slowly reduce the liquid until you have a glaze, about 30 minutes. (This glaze is called a "gastrique," a combination of sweet and acid flavors.) Add the tomatoes, shallots, and onion, and cook slowly over medium heat, stirring often to prevent burning, until the mixture is almost dry and has come together to form the "marmelade."

To prepare the fish, place the fillets on a plate, and season generously with kosher salt and white pepper. Heat a large sauté pan over high heat until hot, then add enough grapeseed oil to just cover the bottom of the pan. Heat the oil until it just begins to shimmer, but not smoke. Add the fillets, skin side down, and cook until golden brown, 2 to 3 minutes. Turn the fillets over and continue to cook, using a spoon to baste the fillets with the cooking oil, until golden brown, 1 to 2 minutes longer.

To serve, pour a pool of vinaigrette in the center of 4 shallow, rimmed bowls. Place a fillet over the sauce, and spoon some of the "marmelade" on top. Garnish with a sprig of parsley or chervil. Serve immediately. Bon appétit!

Note: To blanch and peel the tomatoes, fill a large bowl with water and ice cubes. Bring a large pot of water to a boil. Remove the core from the tomatoes and, using a fork, plunge each tomato into boiling water for 10 seconds then into the iced water to cool. Peel the skin and cut each tomato in halves.

WINE PAIRING BY THE FRENCH LAUNDRY SOMMELIER
THIS DISH WOULD BE BEST SHOWCASED BY THE WHITE WINES OF
THE NORTHERN RHONE REGION.
A VIOGNIER FROM THE AOC OF CONDRIEU WOULD ALSO BE GREAT,
SUCH AS ANDRE PERRET "COTEAU DUCHERY" 2000.

Mussels Steamed in Pinot Noir

PHILIPPE JEANTY
BISTRO JEANTY

With its robust, earthy flavors and buttery sauce, this dish conjures up images of rural France, where Philippe Jeanty was raised. Mussels have never had it so good, and the sauce just beckons for a generous slice of French bread.

Heat 2 tablespoons of the olive oil and 1 tablespoon of the butter in a wide, deep pan over medium-high heat until hot. Add the shallots, thyme, pepper, and bay leaves, and sauté for 2 minutes, being careful not to let the mixture brown. Add the wine and bring the mixture to a boil. Add the mussels, decrease the heat, cover with a lid, and cook just until the mussels open (discard any that do not open). Remove the pan from the heat. Use a slotted spoon to transfer the mussels to individual bowls, reserving the cooking liquid in the pan. Set the pan back on the heat. Add the garlic, parsley, butter, the remaining 2 tablespoons of butter, and the remaining 1 tablespoon of olive oil, stir until the butter is melted, and season to taste with salt. Pour the sauce over the mussels. Serve with toasted bread that has been brushed with olive oil and rubbed with a garlic clove.

CLASSIC: PINOT NOIR OR AGED CHARDONNAY
ADVENTUROUS: SPARKLING ROSÉ

SERVES 8

3 tablespoons extra virgin olive oil

3 tablespoons unsalted butter

2 shallots, finely diced

12 sprigs thyme

2 teaspoons freshly cracked black pepper

8 bay leaves

3 cups Pinot Noir

4 pounds fresh mussels, such as Prince Edward or Mediterranean, scrubbed and debearded

2 tablespoons chopped fresh garlic

2 tablespoons chopped fresh parsley

Salt

1 baguette, cut diagonally into 8 pieces

1 to 2 cloves garlic, halved

ALFONSO NAVARRO
COMPADRES BAR AND GRILL

SERVES 2

4 tablespoons olive oil

8 ounces boneless chicken breast, skin removed and sliced into strips

8 medium scallops

Aztec Spice Blend

1 guajillo chopped pepper or pinch of saffron (optional)

1 teaspoon chopped fresh garlic

10 large uncooked prawns, peeled and deveined

Freshly cut kernels of 2 ears of corn

1/4 cup finely chopped red onion

1 green onion, white and green parts, chopped

3 tablespoons seeded, chopped green chile, or to taste

1/2 teaspoon achiote paste, dissolved in 1 1/2 cups water

1 cup cooked long-grain rice

Fresh cilantro, chopped, for garnish

Avocado slices, for garnish

Roma tomatoes, diced, for garnish

Old Pueblo Sauté

This dish is one of Compadres's most treasured originals and the favorite of many locals. Its relaxed and abundant presentation is reflective of the mood that encompasses Compadres, and the flavors are rich in Aztec heat. This recipe is for two hearty servings, but simply keep multiplying it if you want to make it for a group.

Heat 2 tablespoons of the olive oil in a large nonstick sauté pan over medium-high heat until hot. Add the chicken and sauté until just cooked through, about 4 to 6 minutes. Transfer to a plate and keep warm. Add another tablespoon of the olive oil to the pan, then add the scallops and a pinch of the spice blend, and sauté until just cooked, but still plump and tender. Transfer to the plate and keep warm. Add the remaining tablespoon of olive oil to the pan, then add the guajillo pepper and sauté until crispy. (If you are using saffron, add it with the rice.) Add the garlic and prawns to the pepper, and cook for 10 to 15 seconds while shaking the pan. Add the corn, red and green onions, green chile, and 2 tablespoons of the spice blend. Cook for 10 to 15 seconds while shaking the pan. Add the achiote, decrease the heat to low, and simmer until the liquid is reduced by about half. Add the sautéed chicken and scallops and the rice, mix well, and cook just until heated through.

Serve immediately in large, shallow bowls, garnished with cilantro, avocado, and tomato.

CLASSIC: RIESLING
ADVENTUROUS: SANGIOVESE

AZTEC SPICE BLEND

This is a blend of spices made by Compadres and used in many of their dishes. You can make as much or as little as you want by combining equal quantities of salt, black pepper, chile powder, oregano, granulated garlic, paprika, celery salt, ground ginger, and ground cumin. Store in a sealed jar in a cool dry place.

ACHIOTE PASTE

This is a paste available in Mexican stores and some supermarkets. If you're unable to find it, you can substitute a mixture of 1 1/4 cup chicken stock, 1/4 cup tomato paste, and 1/2 teaspoon vinegar.

Crab and Peach Salad in Radicchio Cups

The colors and textures of this dish are stimulating to the palate as well as the eyes. The combination of the deep red, crisp radicchio, the white, tender crab, the orange, sweet peach, and the green, crunchy cucumber makes for a beautiful and delicious composition. You can also use endive cups instead of radicchio or mango in place of the peach—whatever appeals to you. This is an easy dish to prepare for a relaxed, light luncheon.

To prepare the dressing, whisk together the lemon juice, olive oil, and buttermilk in a small bowl.

To prepare the salad, combine the crab, onion, cucumber, peach, and cilantro in a medium bowl. Add the dressing, toss well, and season to taste with pepper. Spoon the crab mixture onto the radicchio leaves and arrange on a platter. Serve immediately with a sliced baguette.

CLASSIC: YOUNG SPARKLING BLANC DE BLANCS
ADVENTUROUS: PINOT BLANC OR DRY ROSÉ

SERVES 4 TO 6

Dressing

Juice of 1 lemon

2 tablespoons extra virgin olive oil

2 tablespoons buttermilk (optional)

8 ounces fresh crabmeat or canned chunk-style, drained

1/2 red onion, finely diced

1/2 cup finely diced English cucumber

1 peach, diced

1/4 cup chopped fresh cilantro

Freshly ground black pepper

1 large or 2 small heads radicchio, leaves separated, rinsed, and patted dry

1 baguette, sliced, as accompaniment

SERVES 4

Taco Dressing

¹/₄ cup red wine vinegar

2 tablespoons olive oil

¹/₄ small yellow onion, chopped

2 cloves garlic

2 tablespoons chopped fresh
   cilantro

¹/₂ teaspoon Mexican oregano

Salt and freshly ground black pepper

Avocado-Tomatillo Sauce

1 medium avocado, peeled and
   pitted

1 serrano pepper

5 canned tomatillos

2 cloves garlic

2 green onions, white and green
   parts, chopped

4 sprigs cilantro

Salt and freshly ground black pepper

Pasilla Chile Aioli

1 dried pasilla chile (also known
   as ancho chile)

2 cloves garlic

2 tablespoons mayonnaise

2 tablespoons sour cream

Salt and freshly ground white pepper

12 ounces salmon fillets (or any
   firm-fleshed fish) skin and bones
   removed (see note)

Aztec Spice Blend (see page 78)

2 tablespoons olive oil

1 cup shredded green and red
   cabbage

8 fresh corn tortillas

Salmon Tacos with Avocado-Tomatillo Sauce and Pasilla Chile Aioli

I can't pass up these fish tacos when I eat at Compadres. They also prepare them with swordfish, but I prefer the moist, rich salmon combined with the crisp salad and spicy dressings. Most of the unusual ingredients can be found in the Mexican section of many supermarkets, or at specialty Mexican stores.

To prepare the dressing, place the vinegar, olive oil, onion, and garlic in a food processor or blender, and purée. Transfer the mixture to a bowl, add the cilantro and oregano, and mix well. Season to taste with salt and pepper; set aside.

To prepare the sauce, place the avocado, pepper, tomatillos, garlic, green onions, and cilantro in a food processor or blender, and purée. If the mixture is too thick, add just enough water to achieve the desired consistency. Season to taste with salt and pepper; set aside.

To make the aioli, roast the chile over an open flame, such as a gas burner, until the skin starts to blacken. Transfer the chile to a small bowl, add water to cover, and soak for 15 minutes. Place the chile in a food processor or blender. Add the garlic and small increments of water, and purée to form a smooth paste. Transfer the paste to a nonreactive bowl, add the mayonnaise and sour cream, and mix well. Season to taste with salt and pepper; set aside, or cover with plastic wrap and refrigerate until ready to use.

To cook the fish, rub the fillets with enough of the spice blend to coat evenly. Heat the olive oil on a griddle or in a large sauté pan over high heat until hot. Add the fillets and cook for 1 to 2 minutes, then turn and cook for about 1 minute longer for medium-rare (which will be the most tender and moist).

To finish the dish, toss the cabbage with enough of the taco dressing to just coat the leaves. Heat a griddle or a nonstick pan over medium heat. Place the tortillas in stacks of 2 on the griddle and heat until warm, turning them together to heat the other side. Divide the cabbage mixture among the 8 tortillas, top with the salmon, and spoon over the sauce and aioli. Place the tacos on a serving platter, and serve immediately.

Note: To remove bones from salmon fillets, use clean eyebrow or other flat-edged tweezers. First, rub your finger down the spine of the fish to expose the bone ends, then pull them out with the tweezers, or with strong fingers.

CLASSIC: SAUVIGNON BLANC
ADVENTUROUS: GAMAY BEAUJOLAIS

ALFONSO NAVARRO, COMPADRES BAR AND GRILL

At first, Alfonso Navarro was a little reluctant about moving from Honolulu to the Napa Valley where he was offered the chance of opening a new Compadres in Yountville. He and his family had come to love their way of life in Hawaii. At the same time, he recognized the opportunity to make a niche for a Compadres in a town of world-class chefs.

Fortunately for Yountville, he chose to follow his instincts and inject fun, family atmosphere, and classic Compadres spicy, Southwestern flavors into a pivotal location in the heart of the town.

Since that time, Alfonso has grown to appreciate what being in Yountville has meant to both his personal life and his work as a chef. He has found that local and visiting diners are more adventurous and discerning. This has allowed him to be more creative than in other Compadres locations; to experiment with more unusual flavors, one of his favorite pastimes.

Alfonso's sense of well-being is founded in his strong family life, and in keeping fit with racquetball and weights—an activity that has freed him of chronic back pain. A day of bliss for Alfonso is to take his family on an active day trip, whether it's to see the city sights or go on a country drive.

FIDENCIO RIVERA, LAKESIDE GRILL

This shy, talented chef sees his life as "a fortunate one." Coming straight to the Napa Valley from Mexico, he considers this area to be the best place in the United States he could live.

Fidencio is grateful for the many opportunities that living in Yountville has brought him and he credits his mentor, Philippe Jeanty, for much of his knowledge and success. It was under the direction of Philippe that he learned the importance of taking one step at a time to fully master his trade and of having the patience to fully learn a skill before moving on to the next. Even now, Fidencio still marvels at the access he has to Yountville's diverse range of quality chefs who have offered him their friendship and support.

To rejuvenate and get a change of scenery, Fidencio walks out the door onto the golf course for a game, or ventures a little further afield for a day of wine tasting. But still, he insists, for the ultimate therapy, nothing can surpass cooking a meal for his family, expanding their boundaries with new flavors.

Grilled Albacore Tuna Salad

FIDENCIO RIVERA
LAKESIDE GRILL

The Lakeside Grill is surrounded by Yountville's beauty and is the perfect place to enjoy a meal while watching the ducks paddle by. To accompany the view, Fidencio Rivera serves his signature simple yet flavorful food. This fresh, robust entrée salad is a favorite of the Grill's menu, and is as colorful as the view from the grill.

To marinate the tuna, combine the grapefruit juice, olive oil, and cumin in a dish. Place the tuna steaks in the marinade, turn to coat well, and marinate in the refrigerator for 10 minutes. (Don't marinate the fish for much longer, because the acid from the juice will "cook" the fish).

To prepare the salad, combine the pineapple, tomato, onion, cilantro, jalapeño, and orange juice in a medium bowl, toss well, and season to taste with salt and pepper; set aside.

Heat a grill pan to medium-high and brush with oil. Place the tuna steaks on the grill pan, and grill until browned but rare in the center, 1 to 2 minutes per side. Place the salad on individual plates, top with the tuna, and garnish with cilantro. Serve immediately.

CLASSIC: CHARDONNAY
ADVENTUROUS: BARBERA

SERVES 4

Marinade

3 tablespoons freshly squeezed grapefruit juice

2 tablespoons extra virgin olive oil

1 teaspoon ground cumin

4 (1-inch-thick) albacore tuna steaks

Salad

$^1/_2$ cup diced fresh pineapple

$^1/_4$ cup diced vine-ripened tomato

$^1/_4$ cup diced red onion

$^1/_4$ cup chopped fresh cilantro

1 jalapeño, seeded and chopped

$^1/_4$ cup freshly squeezed orange juice

Salt and freshly ground black pepper

Cilantro leaves, for garnish

Meat and Poultry

Rack of Lamb Chandon, page 86

ERIC TORRALBA
DOMAINE CHANDON

(

SERVES 4

Fig and Eggplant Jam

1/2 cup Domaine Chandon
    Pinot Noir
1 cup sugar
4 large fresh figs, peeled
1/2 cup peeled, diced eggplant

2 to 3 cloves garlic
1/4 cup extra virgin olive oil
12 to 16 chops of lamb, divided
    into about 3 chops per person
1 bunch dried thyme
Salt and freshly ground white pepper

For the Fire

1 bundle dried grapevines
1 bunch thyme
1 head garlic

Rack of Lamb Chandon

Eric Torralba brought to Domaine Chandon a secret he used in France and a technique ideal for Napa Valley and his winery-based restaurant. He barbecues meat and fish over a fire made from dried grapevines, which impart an earthy and slightly herbaceous flavor; he also adds fresh thyme and garlic to the fire. The smoke complements the subtle sweetness of the lamb rather than overpowering it.

To prepare the jam, combine the wine and sugar in a large, heavy saucepan over medium heat and bring to a boil. Decrease the heat, add the figs and eggplant, and simmer until thick and syrupy, about 20 minutes. Let cool to room temperature, place in a glass bowl or jar, and set aside or refrigerate until ready to use. (Store any leftover jam, covered and refrigerated, for up to one month, to serve on bread or crackers.)

To prepare the lamb, combine the olive oil and garlic and brush the mixture over the lamb using the thyme as a brush. Season well with salt and pepper.

To prepare the barbecue, place the grapevines in the pit or barbecue and set them on fire. When the flames die down and only red coals remain, add the dried thyme and garlic. Oil the grill and set it over the pit or barbecue. Place the lamb racks, meat side down, on the grill, and cook for 3 to 4 minutes. Turn and cook 3 to 4 minutes longer for medium-rare, or longer if desired. Move the meat to a cool part of the grill or transfer to a serving plate, and let rest for 10 minutes before serving. Cut the lamb into about three-chop portions for each plate.

To serve, place a generous spoonful of jam on each plate and top with the lamb chops.

WINE PAIRING BY DAVID BRIDGES, WINE CAPTAIN, DOMAINE CHANDON
CLASSIC: PINOT NOIR
ADVENTUROUS: CHANDON BLANC DE NOIRS

(

Balsamic and Red Wine Beef with Pumpkin Purée

With a rich red-wine glaze covering slices of tender beef and creamy mashed pumpkin, this dish is classic comfort food. For the most tender beef, take care not to overcook, and serve medium-rare.

Preheat the oven to 350°F.

To prepare the glaze, combine the wine, vinegar, sugar, and rosemary in a small saucepan over high heat, and bring to a boil. Decrease the heat and reduce the mixture until slightly thickened, about 15 to 20 minutes. Remove the rosemary sprig and discard, cover the pan with a lid, and keep warm.

To prepare the beef, brush the fillet with the olive oil and season with pepper. Heat a nonstick grill pan or large nonstick sauté pan over high heat until hot. Add the fillet and sear all sides until browned. Transfer the fillet to an ovenproof dish, cover with foil, and place in the oven. Bake for 8 to 10 minutes for medium-rare. Let the meat rest for 5 minutes before slicing to desired thickness.

While the beef is cooking, prepare the pumpkin purée. Place the pumpkin in a large pan, add enough water to cover, and salt to taste. Bring to a boil over high heat, then decrease the heat and simmer until tender, about 10 minutes. Drain well, then transfer the pumpkin to a large bowl and mash until smooth, adding a little milk or stock if you prefer a creamier mash. Add the nutmeg and season to taste with pepper.

To serve, divide the pumpkin purée among 4 plates and arrange the beef slices over the purée. Drizzle with the glaze and garnish with arugula.

CLASSIC: MERLOT

ADVENTUROUS: CHARDONNAY

SERVES 4

Glaze

1 cup red wine, such as Shiraz, Merlot, or Bordeaux

1/2 cup balsamic vinegar

2 teaspoons sugar

1 sprig rosemary

20 to 22 ounces lean beef fillet, trimmed

1 tablespoon extra virgin olive oil

Freshly ground black pepper

Pumpkin

3 cups peeled, seeded, and chopped pumpkin

Salt

1/2 teaspoon nutmeg

Freshly ground black pepper

Baby arugula leaves, for garnish

Goat Cheese-Filled Chicken Chop with Pancetta on Arugula, Sweet Corn, and New Potato Salad

This recipe calls for "airline" chicken breasts, an industry term for a boneless, skinless breast with the wing bone still attached. It looks like a chicken chop, and your butcher can prepare it for you. Peter Hall's dish introduces a rich flavor to the chicken by adding a crisp pancetta crust—made with pancetta he cures himself—and a smooth filling of goat cheese. Sitting on a simple fresh bed of peppery arugula, potatoes, and sweet corn, this dish captures quintessential Italian country cooking—except from Yountville.

Preheat the oven to 350°F.

To prepare the chicken, lay the chicken breasts flat on a board. Using a sharp knife, make a 2-inch-wide and 2-inch-deep horizontal cut in the thickest part of the chicken to form a small pocket for the goat cheese. Place the cheese in a small bowl, stir to soften, and season to taste with salt and pepper. Place a heaping tablespoon of the cheese in each pocket, taking care not to overstuff or it will come out during cooking. Wrap each breast with 2 pancetta slices, covering in a single spiraling layer.

Heat a large ovenproof nonstick sauté pan over medium heat until hot, then add enough olive oil to cover the bottom of the pan in a thin layer. Carefully place the chicken in the pan, flesh side down, and cook until golden brown, about 2 minutes, lifting occasionally with a spatula so it doesn't stick. Turn the chicken, place the pan in the oven, and cook for about 15 minutes, until cooked through. Remove the pan from the oven and let the chicken rest for 10 minutes.

Meanwhile, prepare the salad. Place the arugula in a large bowl and toss with the corn and potatoes. Add the lemon juice and olive oil, and toss well. Season to taste with salt and pepper.

To serve, divide the salad among 4 plates, and place a chicken chop, either whole or sliced, over the salad. Serve immediately.

CLASSIC: PINOT GRIGIO
ADVENTUROUS: CABERNET FRANC

SERVES 4

4 (8-ounce) "airline" chicken breasts
4 ounces soft goat cheese
Salt and freshly ground black pepper
8 thin slices pancetta, trimmed of excess fat
Extra virgin olive oil for cooking

Salad

2 handfuls baby arugula leaves
Freshly cut corn kernels from 2 ears corn
12 small new potatoes, blanched and halved
Juice of 1/2 lemon
1/3 cup extra virgin olive oil
Sea salt and freshly ground black pepper

☾

SERVES 4

Polenta

2 cups vegetable stock (page 22),
    chicken stock (page 23), or
    water
1 3/4 cups heavy whipping cream
4 shavings fresh nutmeg
1 tablespoon extra virgin olive oil
    or unsalted butter
2 teaspoons salt
3/4 cup polenta
1/2 cup finely grated Parmesan
    cheese

2 (2 1/2-pound) whole rabbits
Chile Sauce (recipe follows), as
    accompaniment
1/2 cup toasted slivered almonds,
    for garnish (see note)
1/4 cup minced fresh chives, for
    garnish

Note: To toast the almonds, place
them in a skillet over medium-high
heat. Toss them continuously in the
skillet until they begin to turn a light
golden color. Transfer the almonds
to a plate and spread them out in a
single layer to cool.

Chile Rabbit with Grilled Polenta

The atmosphere at Mustards Grill suggests good food and comfort, and this dish is about as comfortable as it gets. The rabbit is melt-in-your-mouth tender, the chile sauce brings a hearty warmth to the dish, and a rich bed of polenta soaks it all up. For those who have never dared to cook rabbit, try preparing this dish as Cindy leads you step-by-step and makes it wonderfully simple.

To prepare the polenta, combine the stock, cream, nutmeg, olive oil, and salt in a large saucepan over high heat, and bring to a boil. While whisking, slowly add the polenta in a steady stream. Decrease the heat to medium and cook, stirring occasionally, until tender and thick. Stir in the cheese and remove the pan from the heat. Pour the polenta into an oiled 6 x 8-inch pan. Refrigerate for 30 to 40 minutes to chill. When the polenta is chilled, cut it into 4 wedges.

While the polenta is chilling, prepare the rabbit. Cut each rabbit into 6 pieces: remove the front legs as you would the wings of a chicken; remove the back legs and bone the thigh; and trim off the neck and cut the loin in half. (For a fancier presentation, you can bone the two pieces of rabbit loin off the backbone and trim off the belly flap, reserving the bones and flap meat for stock. You'd then put the loin pieces on the grill much later than the leg pieces, as they cook quite quickly.)

Oil the grill and prepare a medium-hot fire, or preheat a gas grill to medium-high.

To finish the dish, grill the rabbit and polenta. Place the front legs on the grill first. When they begin to brown on one side, add the other pieces. Cook, turning as needed, until a nice, even golden brown, about 8 to 10 minutes. (Remember that you are working with skinless meat without much fat, so it can dry out if cooked too long or on too high a flame.) Transfer to a plate and cover to keep warm.

Next, brush the polenta wedges on both sides with olive oil and place on the grill. Grill, turning each piece one-quarter turn to mark evenly and heat through.

To serve, place a polenta wedge in the center of each plate, arrange 3 pieces of rabbit around the polenta, and top with some of the chile sauce. Garnish with almonds and chives.

CHILE SAUCE

In a medium saucepan over medium heat, combine the stock and chile paste, and bring to a boil. Skim the surface for impurities. Remove the pan from the heat and set aside. In a medium pan over medium-high heat, melt 2 tablespoons of the butter. Add the peppers and cook just to warm through, then add the salt and pepper. Add the stock mixture to the peppers and continue to cook over medium-high heat until the sauce has reduced by about two-thirds. Add the remaining 2 tablespoons of butter, cover with a lid, and keep warm until ready to use.

CHILE PASTE

Preheat the oven to 350°F. Place the chiles on a baking sheet and toast them in the oven for 4 to 6 minutes, until aromatic and a bit crisp. (Take care not to overheat the chiles or burn them.) Place the toasted chiles in a small saucepan and add just enough water to cover. Pour off the water into a container and reserve. Combine the chiles, vinegar, oregano, bay leaf, garlic, paprika, and cayenne in a food processor or blender, and process to a smooth paste, adding as much of the reserved water as needed to bring the paste to the consistency of ketchup. Store the paste in a sealed container in the refrigerator until ready to use. (Use any leftover sauce in marinades or other sauces—it's a great enhancement to store-bought barbecue sauce.)

CLASSIC: MERLOT OR SYRAH
ADVENTUROUS: ROUSANNE

Chile Sauce

4 cups chicken stock (page 23)
1/2 cup chile paste (recipe follows)
4 tablespoons unsalted butter
3/4 cup roasted, peeled, seeded, and chopped red bell peppers
1/2 teaspoon salt
1/4 teaspoon freshly ground black pepper

Chile Paste

6 guajillo chiles, stemmed and seeded
1 1/2 tablespoons distilled white vinegar
2 tablespoons minced fresh oregano
1 bay leaf
2 teaspoons minced fresh garlic
1 1/2 tablespoons paprika
Pinch of cayenne pepper

CINDY PAWLCYN, MUSTARDS GRILL

In 1979, Cindy was working in San Francisco when she was offered the opportunity to come to the Napa Valley to open Meadowood. She fell in love with the area even though, at the time, there were very few restaurants.

A woman of vision and energy, Cindy decided there was a niche for a "clubby," fun food location with good prices that at the same time offered great service. She wanted people to be able to come in their winemaking boots or dressed for business, and for both to feel totally comfortable. And at Mustards, this certainly is the case.

Her food can be captured in just a few words—quality organic produce, fresh, Californian, authentic with modern twists, and no fusion. She makes simplicity seem like a five-star experience and her diversity shows in the different restaurants she owns, each keeping their own distinct flavor and charm—and all with approachable and professional service.

Cindy calls Yountville "a chefs heaven," with its access to local gardens and farms, specialty growers of produce, and wonderful wineries. She finds the town has a great convergence of people and, as a business town, is very cooperative—an important consideration for a chef/owner.

For fitness and leisure, Cindy works out regularly and spends a lot of time gardening. But the real spark comes from a morning kayak, a must before work. It's no wonder Cindy has such energetic radiance!

Chicken Kiev with Garlic Mashed Potatoes

FIDENCIO RIVERA
LAKESIDE GRILL

SERVES 6

After a strenuous game of golf, diners at the Lakeside Grill often feel they've earned Fidencio's version of Chicken Kiev, which sits on a reviving bed of garlic mashed potatoes with a creamy mushroom sauce.

Preheat the oven to 400°F. Oil a baking sheet.

To prepare the potatoes, place the potatoes in a large saucepan, add enough cold water to cover, and bring to a boil over high heat. Lower the heat and simmer until tender. Drain well. Add the garlic and milk, and mash until smooth. Season to taste with salt and pepper. Cover with a lid and keep warm until ready to serve.

To prepare the sauce, heat the olive oil in a shallow frying pan over medium-high heat. Add the mushrooms and garlic, and sauté until the mushrooms are soft, about 2 to 3 minutes. Add the whipping cream and cook, stirring often, until slightly thickened, about 5 minutes. Keep warm until ready to serve.

To prepare the filling, combine the spinach, butter, green onions, and garlic in a medium bowl, and mix well. Season to taste with salt and pepper; set aside.

To prepare the chicken, open the butterflied breasts and place them on a flat work surface. Divide the filling among the breasts, placing it in the center. Starting at either side, roll up the filled breast and tie with string. Place the chicken on the prepared pan. Bake for 10 to 15 minutes, until thoroughly cooked inside. (Test by inserting the point of a sharp knife into the center of the chicken; the juices should run clear and there should be no pink flesh.) Keep warm.

To serve, slice the chicken diagonally in half. Spoon some of the sauce onto a plate, top with a mound of mashed potato, and arrange the chicken over the potatoes.

Garlic Mashed Potatoes

8 medium white potatoes, peeled and diced

2 cloves garlic, crushed

1/2 cup milk or half-and-half

Salt and freshly ground black pepper

Mushroom Sauce

2 tablespoons extra virgin olive oil

4 large, white mushrooms

1 teaspoon crushed garlic

1/2 cup heavy whipping cream or milk

Filling

2 cups chopped fresh spinach

1 tablespoon unsalted butter

2 tablespoons chopped green onions, white and green parts

1 tablespoon crushed fresh garlic

Salt and freshly ground black pepper

6 (7-ounce) skinless chicken breasts, butterflied

CLASSIC: CHARDONNAY
ADVENTUROUS: ZINFANDEL

Grilled Venison with Teleme Cheese Risotto and Blackberry Sauce

JUDE WILMOTH
NAPA VALLEY GRILLE

The piquant sweetness of the blackberry sauce and the rich creamy risotto are the perfect contrast to the lean and mildly gamey venison.

To marinate the venison, place the steaks in a large dish. Add the olive oil and herbs, and season well with salt and pepper. Turn to coat, cover with plastic wrap, and marinate in the refrigerator for at least 2 hours, or overnight. Just before grilling the venison, drain well, removing the excess oil, and set on a plate.

To make the sauce, heat the butter in a large sauté pan over medium heat until melted. Add the shallots and sauté until browned. Add the blackberries and chicken stock, decrease the heat, and reduce until slightly thickened, 8 to 10 minutes. Add the pepper. Keep warm.

Oil the grill and prepare a medium-hot fire, or preheat a gas grill or grill pan to medium-high.

To prepare the risotto, heat the 3 tablespoons olive oil in a large saucepan over medium-low heat until hot. Add the onions and bay leaves and sweat for 1 to 2 minutes. Add the rice and sauté until all the grains are well coated with oil, 1 to 2 minutes. Add the wine and cook, stirring continuously, until all the liquid is absorbed. Add half of the stock and simmer, stirring occasionally, until the liquid is absorbed. Continue adding the stock, a ladle at a time, stirring often and allowing the liquid to absorb before each addition. When all the liquid is absorbed and the rice is tender and creamy, about 20 minutes, remove the bay leaf. Cover the pan with a lid, remove from the heat, and let sit while you grill the venison. Just before serving, fold in the butter, Parmesan, Teleme cheese, pepper, and salt to taste then swirl in a final drizzle of olive oil.

To grill the venison, place the steaks on the grill and cook for 2 minutes per side for rare, or 4 to 5 minutes per side for medium-rare. (Rare will be most tender and have the best flavor.) Let the meat rest for 3 to 5 minutes before slicing.

To serve, place a generous spoonful of risotto on individual plates, and arrange venison slices on the side. Spoon the sauce over the venison and around the risotto. Serve immediately.

CLASSIC: MOUVEDRE/MATARO
ADVENTUROUS: FULL-BODIED SPARKLING ROSÉ

SERVES 6

6 (7-ounce) venison leg fillets

Marinade

2 cups extra virgin olive oil
1 bunch fresh thyme, leaves only, chopped
1 bunch fresh oregano, leaves only, chopped
Salt and freshly ground black pepper

Sauce

2 tablespoons unsalted butter
1 tablespoon chopped shallots
2 cups blackberries
1/2 cup chicken stock (page 23)
Pinch of freshly ground black pepper

Risotto

3 tablespoons extra virgin olive oil, plus extra for drizzling
1/4 cup finely diced yellow onion
2 bay leaves
3 cups arborio rice
1/2 cup dry white wine
5 cups chicken stock (page 23), kept at a simmer
1 tablespoon butter
1/4 cup freshly grated Parmesan cheese
1/4 cup Teleme cheese, or other soft, tangy cow's-milk cheese, such as Brie or Camembert
Pinch of freshly ground black pepper
Kosher salt

❧

SERVES 4 TO 6

Half of 1 turkey breast, bone and
    skin removed
2 cups apple juice
Salt and freshly ground pepper

Crust

1 pound chicken-apple sausage,
    casings removed
1 small onion, coarsely chopped
1 teaspoon crushed garlic
2 egg yolks
1 teaspoon salt
1 teaspoon Worcestershire sauce
1 tablespoon dried sage
1/2 teaspoon freshly ground black
    pepper
3 tablespoons chopped fresh
    parsley

Sweet-Hot Mustard

1/4 cup light sour cream
1 teaspoon dry mustard
1 tablespoon Dijon mustard
1 tablespoon honey

Turkey Wrapped in a Farci Crust

Kinyon Gordon has a playful and adventurous attitude toward food and always seems to come up with a delectable twist on traditional dishes. In this recipe, he has wrapped turkey stuffing around the outside of a tender turkey breast to create a deliciously savory crust. Marinating the turkey for 12 hours in apple juice adds a subtle sweetness and results in a moist and flavorful slice of meat that is surprisingly simple to prepare.

To marinate the turkey breast, combine the turkey with the apple juice in a nonreactive container, cover with plastic wrap, and refrigerate for at least 12 hours or up to 24 hours. Remove the turkey from the apple juice (discard the juice), and season well with salt and pepper.

To prepare the crust, place the sausage, onion, garlic, egg yolks, salt, Worcestershire sauce, sage, and pepper in a food processor, and process until smooth. Add the parsley and process just until the parsley is incorporated. Transfer the mixture to a bowl, cover with plastic wrap, and refrigerate for 1 hour.

Preheat the oven to 350°F. Grease a baking sheet.

Cut two 18-inch-long sheets of wax paper and brush with oil. Place the sausage mixture on the center of the first sheet of wax paper and cover with the second. Using a rolling pin, roll the mixture out to a size that will wrap around the turkey breast. Remove the top sheet and place the turkey on one end of the mixture. Using the bottom sheet of the paper, wrap the mixture around the turkey, pressing it to form an even layer. Remove the bottom sheet of paper. Press together any gaps in the mixture to seal the edges. Place the turkey on the prepared pan. Roast for 40 minutes, until golden brown and cooked through. To test for doneness, insert the point of a sharp knife into the center of the turkey; the juices should run clear and there should be no pink flesh. Let the turkey rest for 15 minutes before slicing.

While the turkey is roasting, prepare the sweet-hot mustard. Combine all the ingredients in a small bowl, and mix well.

To serve, slice the turkey into 1/2-inch to 1-inch slices, and arrange on a serving platter. Serve warm accompanied by the sweet-hot mustard.

CLASSIC: OFF-DRY RIESLING
ADVENTUROUS: SWEETER SPARKLING WINE

❧

Blackened Mustard Chicken with Raisin-Pear Chutney and Cucumber-Buttermilk Sauce

Raisin-Pear Chutney

1 teaspoon brown or yellow
mustard seeds

2 pears or apples, peeled and
finely diced

1/2 cup raisins

1/4 cup brown sugar

1 teaspoon grated lemon zest

2 tablespoons red wine vinegar

1/2 cup water

Cucumber-Buttermilk Sauce

1/2 cup grated English cucumber

1/2 cup buttermilk or plain yogurt

1 tablespoon freshly squeezed
lime juice

1 teaspoon chopped fresh dill

Blackened Mustard Chicken

4 (7-ounce) boneless, skinless
chicken breasts

2 tablespoons melted butter

1 teaspoon Dijon or honey mustard

2 tablespoons yellow mustard
seeds

1 teaspoon dried thyme

1 teaspoon paprika

1 teaspoon freshly ground black
pepper

1 teaspoon sea salt

Olive oil for searing

Dry white wine or chicken stock
(page 23) for steaming

In Yountville, a highlight of the year is the annual Mustard Festival, initiated by Yountvillian George Rothwell. It's a time of festivity, filled with wine tastings, specialty dinners, and all things surrounding the beloved mustard plant. In honor of the event, I created this dish. To complement the blackened spice of the chicken, I've brought in the sweet tang of a mustard seed–accented chutney made with raisins and pears, and finished it off with a cooling cucumber-buttermilk sauce.

To prepare the chutney, heat the mustard seeds in a heavy saucepan over medium-high heat until they start to pop. Add the pears, raisins, brown sugar, lemon zest, vinegar, and water, and bring to a boil. Decrease the heat and simmer until the liquid is thick and syrupy, 30 to 40 minutes; set aside. (The chutney can be made a day or two in advance and stored in a sealed container in the refrigerator.)

To prepare the sauce, combine the cucumber, buttermilk, lime juice, and dill in a bowl. Cover with plastic wrap and refrigerate for at least 15 minutes to allow the flavors to develop.

Preheat the oven to 350°F.

To prepare the chicken, pat dry and trim off any excess fat. Combine the butter and mustard and brush over the plump side of the breasts. Combine the mustard seeds, thyme, paprika, pepper, and sea salt on a plate. Press the buttered side of the breasts onto the mixture to form an even coat.

Heat a large nonstick sauté pan over high heat until hot, then add enough olive oil to just cover the bottom of the pan. Heat the oil until it just begins to shimmer, but not smoke. Add the breasts, crust side down, and sear to blacken the surface, 2 to 3 minutes. Turn the breasts over and sear for 2 minutes longer, then transfer to a casserole dish. Pour about 1/2 inch white wine or chicken stock into the dish to allow the chicken to steam, then set the pan in the oven. Bake for 25 to 35 minutes, until cooked through.

Serve hot on a bed of rice with the chutney and cucumber sauce on the side.

CLASSIC: NAPA VALLEY MERITAGE (MERLOT, CABERNET FRANC BLEND)

ADVENTUROUS: VIOGNIER

Blues Burger with
Sweet and Spicy Jalapeño Salsa

JULIO GARCIA
PACIFIC BLUES CAFÉ

The popularity of this burger led it to become Pacific Blues's signature dish, hence the name. It's a classic burger with a spicy kick that's great to enjoy with an ice-cold beer.

To prepare the salsa, heat the olive oil in a large saucepan to medium-high. Sauté the peppers until soft, about 5 to 7 minutes. Add the vinegar, sugar, and water and bring to a boil. Decrease the heat and simmer until the mixture is thick and syrupy, about 30 minutes. Season to taste with salt. Let cool, then transfer to a bowl, cover, and refrigerate until ready to use. Any extra can be stored in a sealed container in the refrigerator for up to two weeks.

Oil the grill and prepare a medium-hot fire, or oil and heat a grill pan over medium-high heat just before cooking the burgers.

To prepare the burgers, season the meat well with salt and pepper and shape it into 4 patties. Place the patties on the grill and cook until cooked through and browned, about 3 to 5 minutes per side. During the last minute or so of cooking, top the meat with the cheese and allow it to melt, and grill the inside of the buns until lightly toasted.

To serve, place each patty on the bottom half of a bun and spoon over some of the salsa, then top with tomato, onion, lettuce, and the top half of the bun. Serve immediately.

CLASSIC: SIERRA NEVADA PALE ALE

ADVENTUROUS: ZINFANDEL

SERVES 4

Sweet and Spicy Jalapeño Salsa

1/4 cup olive oil

1/2 pound each red and green jalapeño peppers, stemmed, seeded, ribbed, and sliced

1/2 cup balsamic vinegar

1 1/2 cups sugar

2 1/2 cups water

Salt

2 pounds ground turkey or beef

Salt and freshly ground black pepper

4 tablespoons crumbled blue cheese

4 hamburger buns

Tomato slices, onion slices, and lettuce leaves as accompaniment

Five-Spice Pork and Fig Salad

The aromatic Chinese five-spice powder (a mixture of ground anise, chives, cinnamon, fennel, and pepper), honey, and soy sauce complement the moist sweetness of the pork and figs, while the bed of cilantro and basil seems to just bring it all together with a fresh, aromatic burst of flavor. I added ginger and fresh fennel for a stimulating zip on the palate.

To marinate the pork, trim any excess fat and pat dry. Combine the honey, soy sauce, ginger, and five-spice in a shallow nonreactive dish and mix well. Place the pork in the marinade, turn to coat both sides, cover with plastic wrap, and refrigerate for a minimum of 1 hour or overnight, turning the pork over occasionally while marinating.

Preheat the oven to 350°F.

To prepare the salad, combine the fennel and oregano in a medium bowl, and toss with the lemon juice and olive oil; set aside.

Remove the pork from the marinade, allowing the excess to drip off. Heat a grill pan or large nonstick sauté pan over medium-high heat until hot, then add enough olive oil to just coat the bottom of the pan. Heat the oil until it begins to shimmer, but not smoke. Add the pork and sear until browned, 3 to 4 minutes per side. Transfer the pork to an ovenproof dish, cover with foil, and bake for 5 to 10 additional minutes. Just before serving, slice thinly.

To serve, arrange the cilantro and basil over a serving platter or individual plates. Place the fennel mixture over the herbs, and top with the pork slices. Scatter the figs over the top. Drizzle with a little of the port and serve with a sliced baguette and truffle oil for dipping on the side.

CLASSIC: GEWÜRZTRAMINER
ADVENTUROUS: DOLCETTO

SERVES 4

1 pound lean pork loin, leg steaks, or fillet

Marinade

2 tablespoons honey, at room temperature

2 tablespoons soy sauce

1 teaspoon ground ginger

2 teaspoons Chinese five-spice powder

1 bulb fennel, white part only, finely sliced

2 teaspoons fresh oregano leaves, or 1 teaspoon dried

Juice of 1/2 lemon

2 tablespoons extra virgin olive oil, plus extra for searing

1 large bunch cilantro, coarsely chopped

1/2 bunch basil, leaves torn into small pieces

8 fresh figs, quartered, or substitute with seasonal fruit, such as pears, nectarines, or oranges

Port, for drizzling (optional)

Desserts

Sally's Maple-Banana Bread Pudding, page 104

SALLY GORDON
GORDON'S CAFÉ &
WINE BAR

☙

MAKES ONE 10-INCH BUNDT CAKE

1 loaf day-old pain de mie or
    other rich white bread, cut into
    $1/2$-inch cubes

2 ripe bananas, sliced

$1/4$ cup firmly packed brown sugar

1 cup pure maple syrup

9 eggs

4 cups whole milk

2 teaspoons pure vanilla extract

Sally's Maple-Banana Bread Pudding

The aromas surrounding Sally Gordon's café in the morning are truly tantilizing—and the crowds that fill the space with a warm, friendly buzz are proof that the food doesn't just smell good. This recipe is steeped in Yountville tradition, being a version of a dessert Sally's grandmother and mother made, and was the first recipe Sally served when opening Gordon's.

Preheat the oven to 350°F. Butter a 10-inch Bundt pan.

Place the bread in a single layer on the bottom of the prepared pan, then top with a layer of banana slices. Continue to create alternating layers, ending with a layer of bread; set aside.

In a large bowl, whisk together the sugar, syrup, eggs, milk, and vanilla. Pour the mixture over the bread and bananas, allowing the bread to absorb the liquid. If more liquid is needed, add 1 to 2 more whisked eggs.

Bake for 1 hour, or until a skewer inserted in the center of the pudding comes out clean. Let rest for 15 minutes, then loosen the edges of the pudding with a small rubber spatula and turn onto a large plate.

Slice and serve warm.

A LATE HARVEST RIESLING IS THE IDEAL MATCH FOR
THE MOIST RICHNESS OF THIS CAKE

☙

Chocolate, Date, and Walnut Meringue Cake

This decadent dessert is best enjoyed in small slices. It has a dense, rich texture and crunchy topping, similar to a meringue or macaroon. It is based on a recipe for Italian amaretti, small cookies made with beaten egg whites, sugar, ground nuts, and just a touch of flour. Made into a cake, it has more of a moist center, especially with the added dates. It can be tricky to release the cake from the pan, so be sure to line it well with a circle of parchment cut to fit the base of the pan.

MAKES ONE 9-INCH CAKE

1 1/4 cups walnut pieces
2/3 cup dates
1/4 cup cocoa powder
1/4 cup all-purpose flour
3/4 cup sugar
4 egg whites
Confectioners' sugar, for dusting (optional)

Preheat the oven to 350°F. Lightly grease and flour a 9-inch cake pan, then line the base with a circle of parchment.

Place the walnuts, dates, cocoa, flour, and 1/4 cup of the sugar in a food processor and pulse on and off until the mixture resembles coarse crumbs; set aside.

Place the egg whites in a bowl and whip them with electric beaters until they hold soft peaks. While beating, gradually add the remaining 1/2 cup of sugar and beat until the mixture is thick and glossy. Using a large spoon, gently fold in the walnut mixture just until incorporated. Spoon the mixture into the prepared pan and bake for 20 minutes, or until just set and the top feels like a firm sponge. Place the cake on a wire rack and let it cool in the pan for 5 to 10 minutes, then run a knife around the outside of the cake, turn it out carefully onto the rack, and let cool completely.

To serve, invert the cake onto a serving plate and dust with confectioners' sugar before slicing. Serve each slice with a scoop of vanilla gelato or a dollop of crème fraîche, if desired, or enjoy a slice on its own, straight from the pan.

THE DECADENT RICHNESS OF THIS CAKE
WELCOMES A VINTAGE PORT OR MERLOT

Mango and Prickly Pear Sorbet
with Fortune Cookies

CINDY PAWLCYN
MUSTARDS GRILL

Mustards is as much an institution in Yountville as it is a comfortable, relaxing place to enjoy food. Many of the ingredients come from Cindy's own garden, and the flavors of the food reflect the restaurant's atmosphere—fresh, fun, and adventurous yet simple. Even though prickly pears are most often grown in South America and used in South American cooking, the cacti thrive in the gardens of Mustards, where they are used to add a sweet, tangy, and refreshing touch to salads and many other specials. Here, Cindy uses prickly pears and mangoes to create smooth, rich sorbets that she pairs with fortune cookies.

SERVES 4

Prickly Pear Sorbet

3 pounds ripe prickly pears
   (yellow or red)
1 1/2 cups sugar
1 tablespoon lemon juice

If the spines have not been removed from the prickly pears, be very careful when handling the fruit, and be sure to use gloves. To remove the prickers, hold the fruit with metal tongs under cold running water and scrub the prickers off with a vegetable scrubber. Peel off the outer skin so you reveal the juicy interior. Purée the flesh in a blender or food processor and process until liquefied, then add the sugar and lemon juice. Strain the purée through a fine-mesh strainer. Taste and add more lemon juice or sugar if needed. Freeze in an ice-cream maker according to the manufacturer's directions. Transfer the sorbet to a covered container and place in the freezer until ready to serve.

To make the mango sorbet, combine the sugar and water in a saucepan and stir to dissolve. Bring to a boil, then remove from the heat, peel the skin from the mangoes and remove the seeds. Purée the flesh in a blender or food processor and process until liquefied. Strain the purée through a fine-mesh strainer, and stir in the syrup and lemon juice. Freeze in an ice-cream maker according to the manufacturer's directions.

To prepare the cookies, preheat the oven to 375°F.

In a large bowl, whisk together the egg whites and vanilla. Add the flour, salt, and sugar, and beat until smooth. On a baking sheet, spread tablespoonfuls of the batter into 2-inch circles. Bake for 3 to 4 minutes, just until golden brown. Remove the pan from the oven and, working quickly while the cookies are still warm, use a spatula to remove them from the pan, then place a fortune inside and fold immediately.

Mango Sorbet

1 1/2 cups sugar
1 1/2 cups water
3 pounds ripe mangos, peeled and
   seeded (about 4 mangoes)
2 teaspoons freshly squeezed
   lemon juice

Fortune Cookies

MAKES ABOUT 25 COOKIES

8 egg whites
1 teaspoon pure vanilla extract
1 cup flour
1 teaspoon salt
2 cups sugar

TRY PAIRING A SUMMERY SPARKLING DEMI-SEC WINE
WITH THESE LIVELY SORBETS

Pear, Merlot, and Olive Oil Cake

MAKES ONE 9-INCH CAKE

2 1/2 cups Merlot or other rich
    red wine

3/4 cup blanched or slivered
    almonds

2 cups flour

2 teaspoons baking powder

1 teaspoon ground cardamom
    (optional)

1 teaspoon cinnamon

4 eggs, separated

1 cup sugar

1 pear, peeled and diced

1 teaspoon pure vanilla extract

1/3 cup extra virgin olive oil

Whipped cream, for garnish
    (optional)

You may think it strange to use extra virgin olive oil in a cake, let alone red wine, but together they add rich fruit flavors, a dense moist texture, and unique color. Merlot is one of Yountville's outstanding varietals, and it adds a rich, deep, and fruity flavor to the cake. I love to serve it for dessert over a swirl of crème anglaise and a glass of dessert wine, but it's equally delicious served as-is with coffee.

Preheat the oven to 350°F. Lightly grease two 9-inch round baking pans with oil and line the bottoms with parchment paper.

In a small saucepan over high heat, bring the wine to a boil. Decrease the heat and simmer for 20 minutes, until reduced to about 3/4 cup. Let cool and set aside 1/4 cup for serving with the cake.

Place the almonds in a food processor and process until finely ground. Sift the almonds with the flour, baking powder, cardamom, and cinnamon into a large bowl, adding any larger pieces of nut that remain in the sieve.

Place the egg yolks and 1/2 cup of the sugar in a food processor, and process until pale and thick. Add the pear and vanilla, and process just until smooth. With the motor running, slowly add the olive oil in a thin stream, and process until smooth. Pour the mixture into the flour mixture, then add the 1/2 cup of reduced wine. Mix gently with a large metal spoon until the ingredients are just incorporated.

Place the egg whites in a bowl and, using an electric mixer, beat on high speed until soft peaks form. While beating, slowly add the remaining 1/2 cup of sugar and beat until stiff and shiny. Lightly fold the egg white mixture into the batter. Pour the batter into the prepared pans and bake for about 20 minutes, until a skewer inserted in the center of the cake comes out clean. Cool in the pans for 10 minutes, then turn the cakes out onto a wire rack and let cool completely.

To serve, spoon some whipped cream onto individual plates, drizzle with a little of the reserved reduced red wine, and top with a slice of the cake.

THIS ITALIAN-STYLE CAKE BECKONS FOR AN EQUALLY
ITALIAN VIN SANTO OR ITALIAN DESSERT WINE

Caramelized Figs

I had the pleasure of having a dinner prepared by Villagio and Vintage Inn's hotel manager, Mary Crowe, while sitting overlooking the vineyards of Yountville on a warm summer evening. To finish the meal, Mary brought out her summer favorite, an exquisitely simple, light, and delicious fig recipe that I begged to include in this book. Figs do have a short window of availability, so when they're not in season, try this with apricots, peaches, kiwi, or your favorite fruit. Use the ingredient measurements as guidelines, but feel free to experiment to your own taste. It's really one of those recipes where it's a sprinkle of this and a splash of that.

Preheat the broiler. Place the figs, cut side up, on a baking pan that will contain the juices, and sprinkle with the vanilla and nutmeg. Broil for 1 to 2 minutes, or until the figs are just starting to soften. Drizzle with the cream (just enough for a thin cover), and broil for another minute longer, or until the figs have caramelized and are starting to brown. Serve immediately in bowls, with any excess juice spooned over the top.

SERVES 4

12 fresh figs, halved
1 teaspoon pure vanilla extract
1 teaspoon ground nutmeg
1/3 cup heavy whipping cream

A RICH, FULL TAWNY PORT OR BLACK MUSCAT
WILL COMPLEMENT THE FRESH FIG FLAVORS

Berry and Moscato-Mascarpone Mille-Feuille

I love this dish for those times when you have friends coming for dinner and feel like serving something a little special for dessert, but want to enjoy your friends rather than the kitchen. I make the pastry triangles a day or two ahead of time and whip the filling before my guests arrive, so all I have to do before serving is assemble and dust with sugar. Try preparing this dessert with any fruit you prefer, such as kiwi fruit, mango, grapes, papaya, peaches, or plums. Moscato is a sweet, fruity dessert wine that adds a fresh note to the creamy mascarpone.

Preheat the oven to 350°F. Line 2 baking sheets with parchment paper.

To prepare the pastry, combine the nuts, sugar, and cocoa in a small bowl. Lay 2 sheets of filo pastry on a clean, dry work surface. Brush the top lightly with melted butter, then scatter with one-half of the nut mixture. Lay another 2 sheets on top and brush with butter. Sprinkle the top with the remaining nut mixture. Cut the stack into 12 triangles or squares and place on the prepared baking sheets. Bake for 10 to 12 minutes, until golden brown. Transfer to a wire rack to cool. The pastry can be prepared 1 to 2 days in advance, and kept stored at room temperature in an airtight container.

To prepare the filling, combine the mascarpone, Moscato, sugar, and orange zest in a medium bowl. Lightly beat the mixture together until the ingredients are combined.

To serve, place a filo triangle on each of 4 plates, then top with a spoonful of the filling and scatter with some of the berries. Add a second layer of filo, filling, and berries, then finish by topping with a final filo triangle. Dust with confectioners' sugar just before serving.

My thanks to Aaron Rodriguez, our welcoming friend at Bistro Don Giovanni's bar (just down the road from Yountville) for the inspiration of adding the Moscato to this dish.

MUSCAT CANELLI WILL BRING OUT THE FLAVOR IN THE MASCARPONE
AND BLEND WONDERFULLY WITH THE FRUIT

SERVES 4

Pastry

- 1/2 cup finely chopped nuts, such as hazelnuts, macadamias, walnuts, or almonds
- 2 tablespoons sugar
- 1 teaspoon cocoa powder
- 4 sheets filo pastry
- 1/3 cup melted unsalted butter

Filling

- 1/2 cup mascarpone cheese
- 2 tablespoons Moscato
- 3 tablespoons confectioners' sugar
- 1 teaspoon grated orange zest

- 2 cups mixed berries, such as blueberries, raspberries, blackberries, and strawberries
- Confectioners' sugar for dusting

SERVES 12

Pâte Sucrée (Tart Shell)

3/4 cup unsalted butter, at room
   temperature
1/3 cup confectioners' sugar
1 egg
Pinch of salt
1 1/2 cups flour

Poached Pears

1 (750-ml) bottle dry white wine,
   such as Sauvignon Blanc
3 cups water
3 cups sugar
6 pears, peeled, stems removed

Sebastien's Tart Mix

1/2 cup unsalted butter
2 eggs
2/3 cup sugar
1/4 cup milk
1/4 cup heavy whipping cream
1/4 cup flour
1/4 cup finely ground almonds

Sliced almonds, lightly toasted
   (see note), for garnish
Crème fraîche, for garnish

Pear Tart

*I can't think of a more delicious indulgence than these recipes
from Bouchon Bakery, delectably French to the core, like their
creator, Sebastien Rouxel. Thankfully, we Yountvillians don't
have to leave home to enjoy a touch of France, and can instead
just stroll down the street.*

To prepare the tart shell, place the butter and confectioners' sugar in
a medium mixing bowl and beat until the mixture becomes light and
fluffy. While beating, add the egg and salt, and beat until well blended.
Using a spoon or spatula, fold in the flour and mix until well incorporated. Wrap the dough in plastic wrap and refrigerate until well
chilled, about 1 hour.

Preheat the oven to 350°F. Lightly butter a 12-inch tart pan with a
removable bottom, then dust with flour until the ring is completely but
very lightly coated.

On a well-floured board, roll the dough out to a thickness of about
1/4 inch. Press the dough into the prepared pan, and refrigerate again
for another 20 minutes to chill. Line the tart shell with parchment
paper, cover it with dried beans to weigh it down, and bake for 20 minutes, until lightly golden brown. Let cool completely.

To poach the pears, combine the wine, water, and sugar in a large
pot over high heat, and bring to a boil. Decrease the heat and simmer
until the sugar dissolves. Remove the pan from the heat, skim the surface for impurities, and let cool. Place the pears in the wine mixture,
set the pan over low heat, and bring to a very low simmer. Simmer for
50 to 60 minutes. Check for doneness by inserting a knife through the
center: if the knife goes through without any resistance, the pears are
ready. Carefully remove the pears from the poaching liquid and place
on a plate. Let cool.

To prepare the tart mix, heat the butter in a small sauté pan over
medium-high heat until golden brown. Remove the pan from the heat
and let cool slightly. In a large bowl, whisk together the eggs and sugar
until well blended. While whisking, slowly add the milk and cream.
Gently fold in the flour and ground almonds. Add the browned butter
and mix just until incorporated; set aside.

To assemble the tart, remove the beans and paper from the cooled
tart shell. Pour enough of the tart mix into the shell to fill it to about
1/4 inch in depth.

Slice each pear in half lengthwise and remove the seeds. Carefully
arrange all twelve halves, split side down, over the filling. Bake for

about 45 minutes, or until lightly golden in color. Remove from the oven and sprinkle with toasted almonds. Slice and serve warm with a dollop of crème fraîche.

WINE PAIRING BY THE FRENCH LAUNDRY SOMMELIER
ALBAN "OECHSLE," EDNA VALLEY ROUSSANE.
THIS IS A VERY RIPE SWEET WINE MADE FROM BOTRYTISED GRAPES.

Note: To toast the almonds, place them in a skillet over medium-high heat. Toss them continuously in the skillet until they begin to turn a light golden color. Transfer the almonds to a plate and spread them out in a single layer to cool.

Mascarpone Sorbet with Coffee Macaroons and Hot Chocolate

SEBASTIEN ROUXEL
BOUCHON BAKERY

These morsels have to be one of the most delectable treats I have ever tasted. Crisp, moist, melt-in-your-mouth macaroons filled with a creamy cool refreshing sorbet, all capped off with truly decadent hot chocolate—it's pure bliss, enjoyed with a huge smile. Now this is my idea of the food I'll be eating in heaven!

To make the sorbet, combine the mascarpone and syrup in a blender, and blend until smooth. Strain through a chinois or fine-mesh sieve. Freeze the sorbet in an ice-cream maker following the manufacturer's instructions. Once the sorbet is frozen, transfer it to a container, add the lemon juice and candied zest, and mix well. Cover the container and place in the freezer until ready to serve. The sorbet will keep for up to 2 days.

Preheat the oven to 500°F. Line a baking sheet with parchment paper.

To prepare the macaroons, place the confectioners' sugar and ground almonds in a food processor, and process until well blended. Sift the mixture through a fine-mesh sieve into a small bowl; set aside. In the bowl of a mixer fitted with the whip attachment, whip the egg whites until they form stiff peaks (be careful not to overwhip, or the whites will break and weep). While beating, slowly add the sugar and coffee extract, just to incorporate. Gently fold the almond mixture into the egg white mixture (be very careful to avoid overmixing, or the meringue will lose too much volume).

Transfer the mixture to a pastry bag fitted with a round tip, and pipe onto the prepared pan into 2-inch circles. Place the pan in the oven and, as soon as you shut the door, decrease the temperature to 350°F. Bake for 8 to 10 minutes, until the macaroons are golden brown. Let cool on the pan and then transfer to a wire rack and use right away. Macaroons will keep for 4 to 5 days in the refrigerator or 4 weeks in the freezer.

To prepare the hot chocolate, heat the milk in a saucepan over medium-low heat until it just comes to a boil. Remove the pan from the heat. Add the chocolate, and stir until smooth. Keep warm until ready to serve.

To finish the dish, place a small spoonful of sorbet on top of a macaroon, then set another cookie on top to form a sandwich. Serve immediately, with hot chocolate.

MAKES ABOUT 25 FILLED
MACAROONS

Sorbet

1 pound mascarpone cheese
2 cups simple syrup (see note)
1/3 cup freshly squeezed lemon
   juice
2 teaspoons minced candied
   lemon zest

Macaroons

3 egg whites
2 tablespoons sugar
3/4 cup confectioners' sugar
3/4 cup ground almonds
1 teaspoon liquid coffee extract
   (available at some supermarkets
   and specialty food stores), or
   1 teaspoon very strong brewed
   espresso, cooled

Hot Chocolate

4 cups whole milk
10 ounces bittersweet chocolate,
   finely chopped

Note: To make simple syrup, combine 2 cups water and 2 cups sugar
in a medium saucepan over high
heat, and bring to a boil. Boil until
the sugar dissolves, about 2 minutes.
Remove the pan from the heat and
let cool completely.

SEBASTIEN ROUXEL, BOUCHON BAKERY AND THE FRENCH LAUNDRY

The eyes of this lively young Frenchman from the Loire Valley sparkle as he looks around his surrounds in Yountville. In this town he has found a location that brings him a sense of closeness to home with its terroir of grapevines and orchards, its abundance of small farms with daily produce, and its wealth of cafes, world-class restaurants, and good food.

To find all this, while also having the honor of working with Thomas Keller as his executive pastry chef for the Bouchon Bakery and The French Laundry, has brought Sebastien and his wife a great sense of joy and contentment. They love the peace and quiet, and the friendliness of their community for their young family.

With the very discerning and knowledgeable diners coming to The French Laundry and the more casual crowd lining up at the Bouchon Bakery, Sebastien gets to put his wonderful French baking skills to full use. He can prepare everything from the ultimate elegant parfait or dessert to a loaf of rustic country French bread.

Sebastien finds relaxation in taking hikes with his wife or a stroll through Yountville with their baby and pet bulldog, and wine tasting is always on the agenda. Sebastien also swears by a regular massage to relieve the aches from constant standing. The ultimate, however, is to take off to the water for long relaxing boat trips, preferably to the East Coast to enjoy his wife's family at the same time.

Rose-Scented Grape Teabread

Rose bushes are almost as much a part of the Napa Valley as grape vines. It was once thought that the roses could be used as detectors of growing problems that could potentially affect the precious vines, but now most are just beautiful decoration. In this recipe I have captured the bounty of both plants in this simplified version of an Italian schiacciata.

Preheat the oven to 400°F. Lightly oil a baking sheet or line with parchment paper.

Sift the flour into a large bowl. Add the sugar and lemon zest, and mix well. Make a well in the center. In a small bowl, whisk together the olive oil, buttermilk, and rosewater, and pour it into the well. Using a knife, mix quickly and gently to form a soft dough. Turn the dough out onto a lightly floured board and knead gently until smooth. Divide the dough in half. Press or roll out each piece of dough to make two 8 to 9-inch rounds. Place one round on the prepared pan. Press one-half of the grapes about halfway into the dough, leaving space between each grape, so they cover the surface. Sprinkle with 2 tablespoons of the sugar and dust lightly with cinnamon. Top with the second round of dough, then nestle the remaining grapes in the valleys between the first layer of grapes. Sprinkle with the remaining sugar and another dusting of cinnamon. Bake for 10 to 15 minutes, until golden brown and the grapes are just caramelized.

Serve warm from the oven, topped with sweetened ricotta or a scoop of your favorite gelato.

THIS DESSERT IS IDEAL SERVED WITH A DRY SHERRY

SERVES 6

- 2 cups self-rising flour
- 2 teaspoons freshly grated lemon zest
- 2 tablespoons sugar
- 1 tablespoon olive oil
- 1 cup buttermilk
- 1 teaspoon rose water (available at most supermarkets and specialty food stores)
- 2 cups mixed seedless grapes
- 1/4 cup firmly packed brown sugar
- 2 teaspoons cinnamon or nutmeg

Wine and Cheese Lovers Guide

A visit to the wine country conjures up images of afternoons spent lingering over a platter of various cheeses served with local wines, especially in fall while breathing in the heady aromas of freshly crushed grapes. Hidden behind the generous cheese counter of Cucina à la Carte at Villagio Inn & Spa is our resident expert on pairing cheese and wine, Kathryn Kenney. In the following pairings, she draws in the elements of not only Napa, but also some of the classic wine regions of France, Italy, and other European countries.

First, Kathryn advises that every person's tastes are different. If you like a certain wine or beer with a certain cheese, by all means, enjoy them together! The ideal way to get the most flavor from cheese is to serve it at room temperature. Also, the rind on most cheeses is edible, although it may be stronger in flavor. So it's up to you whether or not you want to enjoy it. Adding some grapes, nuts, and even honey to your cheese platter gives your taste buds more to reflect on.

Camembert. This French cow's-milk cheese can be either pasteurized or unpasteurized. Either way, Pinot Noir or Gamay wines pair nicely with it.

Explorateur. The ideal complement to this French triple-cream cheese is Champagne and strawberries. If, by chance, you have any left over, try it for breakfast, served on toast with a little honey.

Feta. This simple, yet classic, sheep's-milk cheese is produced in many places around the world, and is sometimes made with cow's milk as well. The original feta was made in Greece and was eaten with a mellow white wine, a great loaf of bread, and some olives.

Fontina Val d'Aosta. This unpasteurized, earthy, and full-flavored cheese is from Italy. To get the most out of this cow's-milk cheese, pair it with a rich red Cabernet. It's perfect for fondues as well as macaroni and cheese.

Goat cheese. What you pair with goat cheese will vary depending on its age. If the cheese is young, try a dry white wine, such as Sauvignon Blanc, Fume Blanc, or Chardonnay. If the cheese has a heavy rind on it as well as some age, a Bordeaux will go nicely.

Gorgonzola. If you are serving this Italian blue cheese as an appetizer or as part of a meal, serve it with a full-bodied red wine such as a Barolo or Chianti. If you are serving it as part of your dessert plate, sliced pears, honey, and a Port or Marsala are the way to go.

Morbier. Light fruity red wines such as Beaujolais will bring out the nutty, fruity flavors of this French cow's-milk cheese. The vegetable ash in the middle separates the morning and evening milks. It adds no additional flavor to the cheese—it just looks nice.

Mozzarella di Bufula. Made with buffalo's milk, this variety is a little sweeter than the cow's-milk mozzarella. It also has more depth of flavor and is a little creamier in texture. Try slices of fresh mozzarella, heirloom tomatoes, and a little fresh basil on a hot summer day. Add a Sauvignon Blanc, a Fumé Blanc, or even a sparkling wine, and you'll be set!

Parmigiano Reggiano. This Italian raw-cow's-milk cheese is renowned for its usage with pasta and rice dishes. But have you ever tried it with simply a great balsamic vinegar? The sweet flavor of the balsamic vinegar and the saltiness of the Parmigiano are wonderful together. Try it on your next cheese platter with a full-flavored red wine such as Chianti or Barbera.

Ricotta. In Italian, ricotta means "recooked." This sheep's-milk product is mild and nutty with a little sweetness that complements other foods. Whether you're serving it with pasta or dessert, choose a wine that complements that particular dish.

Roquefort. This French unpasteurized-sheep's-milk cheese goes equally well with strong reds such as Châteauneuf-du-Pape or sweet white wines like Sauternes. A perfect addition to this pairing would be a nice ripe pear.

Taleggio. This full-bodied Italian cow's-milk cheese is Brie-like in texture but with more flavor. It is a sophisticated cheese that pairs perfectly with a nice Chianti.

Tete de Moine. This unpasteurized cow's-milk cheese from Switzerland calls out for beer! A full-bodied stout or ale is a perfect match. If you must drink wine with your cheese, try any full-flavored red—a nice Hermitage for example.

Everyday Spa

The wonderful food and wine of Yountville and the Napa Valley are, without a doubt, two key factors that make this region a culinary destination and ultimate getaway. But there are other contributing elements within this oasis that are just as important for achieving the ultimate in health, relaxation, and revival. There are the spas, walking tracks with panoramic vistas, tennis courts, a myriad of recreational activities, unique hotels, inns and bed-and-breakfasts, shops, and galleries—it's no wonder the locals clearly enjoy living here and soaking up all that life has to offer.

Within the following pages you will discover ways of bringing health and relaxation to your home, as well as other helpful tips and ideas, so you, too, can experience the most in the simple pleasure of living.

Refreshing Smoothie Recipes, page 125

Blends of Yountville–
Refreshing Smoothie Recipes

Smoothies provide the amount of fruit needed for our daily dose of many vitamins and minerals. And, best of all, they taste great and are refreshing. Experiment with your own favorite fruit combinations.

Basic Smoothie Recipe

All of the following recipes can be prepared as instructed in the Basic Smoothie Recipe.

Combine all of the ingredients in a blender and whirl at top speed for approximately 1 minute, or until smooth. Pour into a glass and enjoy.

A combination of fruits (fresh or frozen) or vegetables

Any combination of the following: juice, milk, rice or soy milk, yogurt, or sorbet

Any additional ingredients the recipe calls for

Ice cubes

WAKE-UP CALL

1 banana, peeled and sliced into 2-inch chunks

1 to 1 1/2 cups orange juice

3 to 4 strawberries

1/4 cup sliced papaya or mango

2 to 3 tablespoons plain yogurt

2 teaspoons wheat germ

Ice cubes

GRAPEFRUIT REFRESHER

1 cup grapefruit juice

1/2 sliced pear

1/2 cup rice milk

3 to 4 slices cantaloupe or watermelon

Ice cubes

ANTIOXIDANT BERRY BLITZ

1 cup red grape or cranberry juice

1/4 to 1/2 cup raspberries or blueberries

1 apricot or a slice of papaya

2 to 3 tablespoons plain yogurt

Ice cubes

CUCUMBER COOLER

1 cup buttermilk or mineral water

1/4 cup grated cucumber

Sprig of mint

Dash of bitters or tabasco (optional)

Ice cubes

Following are recipes from Villagio Inn & Spa:

POOLSIDE SMOOTHIE

3 strawberries

8 blueberries

1 banana, peeled and sliced into 2-inch chunks

3/4 cup cranberry juice

1/4 cup low-fat milk

1/4 cup plain yogurt

1 to 2 teaspoons sugar

Splash of Frangelico (optional)

PEACH WHIP

1 sliced peach

1/4 cup peach yogurt

1 cup orange juice

Sugar to taste

Dash of Cointreau (optional)

Ice cubes

HAWAIIAN PUNCH

1/2 cup diced mango

1/2 cup diced papaya

1 cup pineapple juice

Splash of coconut juice

Ice cubes

JAMAICAN VACATION

1 shot of rum

1/2 cup pineapple juice

1/2 cup cranberry juice

Splash of tonic water

Ice cubes

Pamper Yourself through Giving

Making people happy brings happiness to the giver. And pampering those you love will make you feel just as pampered as if you were the one being spoiled, especially seeing and sharing in their pleasure and joy. Giving is a great way to help others overcome tension or times of difficulty and you'll find your own stress level will go down too.

- After a day's work, greet your loved one with a glass of champagne, their favorite music, and some "sensual" canapes. Try oysters topped with caviar or smoked salmon on a crisp wafer with crème fraîche. Then follow up with a table for two at a favorite restaurant or a partners' massage.

- Buy some aromatic massage oils and give someone you love a long massage, then prepare a luxurious bath accented with burning candles and a glass of wine.

- Just hug someone and tell them how great they are and how much you love them.

- Buy a friendship card for someone for no reason at all.

- Think of something that brings you great pleasure and do the same for someone else.

Antioxidant Power

It's well known that **tomatoes** are a wonderful source of antioxidants, including lycopene. Some researchers say that cooking tomatoes enhances the concentration of lycopene—perhaps the Italians knew this when they based their diet on rich tomato sauces.

Following are some more examples of foods rich in nature's phytochemicals and antioxidants—those elements in food that help protect us from disease—and some tips for using them to bring pleasure into daily meals.

Ruby grapefruit and watermelon contain the same element as tomatoes. Try adding sliced ruby grapefruit to a salad with mixed greens and avocado. Or use the juice to make a delicious salad dressing. Finish a meal with some fresh or frozen watermelon—it's nature's ice cream.

Yellow and orange fruits and vegetables, such as **pumpkins, carrots, yams, mangos, oranges, and papaya,** are full of antioxidants. Enjoy a big bowl of the Pumpkin and Apple Soup (page 18) or try roasted carrots and yams tossed with greens for a warm salad along the lines of the Roasted Mixed Potato and Arugula Salad (page 29). Cubed mango and papaya make a wonderful addition to a salsa with cilantro, tomato, and cucumber. Try serving yellow and orange fruits and vegetables with grilled fish, prawns, or chicken.

Don't forget deep green leafy vegetables, such as **spinach, dandelion leaves, arugula, and basil.** Wilt a selection of dark green leaves in seasoned white wine or water, then toss with pasta or blend with cooked potatoes for a thick, flavorful soup addition.

Wine and grapes are simple to get into your diet—and just look at the French and their longevity! Cook grapes in red wine and reduce to make a thick sauce. Wine makes a wonderful cooking base for all kinds of dishes—risottos, stews, poached meats, fruit, and even baked goods, such as the Pear, Merlot, and Olive Oil Cake (page 108). Or just freeze grapes for a summer cooler—kids love them.

Apples and green and black tea are rich in flavonoids. Enjoy a morning cup of tea with an apple to wake up.

Soy foods, beans, and lentils add fiber and protein to your diet and are a great addition to any meal. Puree white beans with potatoes to create a light, creamy base for grilled meat, casseroles, and

fish. Or marinate tofu in teriyaki sauce and grill, then layer with blanched mushrooms and spinach for an Asian lasagna.

Cranberries, raspberries, blueberries, eggplant, beets, red grapes, and other blue and purple plant foods are delicious additions to your diet. Try Philippe Jeanty's Beet and Mâche Salad (page 30) or cook berries in wine and add sugar or balsamic vinegar to create either a sweet or savory sauce. Grilled or roasted eggplant pureed with garlic and lemon juice makes a great dip or spread.

Broccoli and Brussels sprouts are great simply roasted or steamed. Toss with extra virgin olive oil and toasted pecans for a yummy side dish.

And the wonderfully aromatic **garlic, onion, leek, and chives** also have a range of therapeutic properties and need no instruction on use—they simply add great flavor to just about anything savory.

Pampering Body Recipes— Fruit for Your Body and Soul

Avocado Passion

Avocado is not only a delicious and healthy alternative to spread on bread or make into a creamy sauce, it is also rich in monoun-saturated fats—the same kind found in olive oil, which is given much of the credit for the health of the Mediterranean diet. Avo-cados are also a good source of vitamins A, E, some B group, and folate, as well as potassium, iron, zinc, and fiber. Maybe that's why they also make a wonderful pampering body scrub and skin treatment and have been used this way for centuries. Try this lux-urious body polish, a great one for when avocados are at their peak in season.

Mash the flesh of 2 to 3 avocados with a squeeze of fresh lemon juice and a few tablespoons of oatmeal. Blend the ingredients together to form a paste. Rub the paste all over your body, especially those parts that could do with an extra emollient treatment, such as elbows and hands. Work the avocado mixture into your skin well and, if you have time, wrap yourself in an old, clean sheet and lie down for half an hour for a total pampering experience. (Make sure you have a cup of tea to sip while you soak up the hydrating properties.) Afterward, sink into a hot bath and gently massage the avocado cream into your skin, then rinse off in a warm shower.

Papaya Smoother

Another tropical fruit with a realm of health benefits is papaya or, as known in the Pacific, pawpaw. Not only is it a rich source of vitamin C and antioxidants, it contains the enzyme papain, which is particularly helpful for digestion. Papaya makes a won-derful partner with a squeeze of lime juice for a delicious break-fast. When I was travelling in Fiji, I learned that the Fijians feed it to their babies as one of their first solid foods and also smooth it over their skin for its softening qualities. It works as a mild, nourishing exfoliant.

Make your own papaya facial mask by mashing the flesh of a papaya with a squeeze of fresh lime juice and a few spoonfuls of plain yogurt. Smooth the mixture over your face or any body parts you'd like to soften. Leave it on for 10 to 20 minutes while your skin reaps the benefits. Slip into a hot bath or shower and rinse.

Our ancestors have much to offer us as they didn't have the benefit of the myriad of potions and lotions we have at our fingertips today. Here are a couple of examples.

Fruits of the Vine Soak

It's not only the French that reap the health benefits from a daily glass or two of wine. It appears that the Chinese have long used wine in a slightly different way—for soaking in to balance and purify the skin.

For the ultimate in pampering, pour a glass of white wine for yourself and pour the rest into the bath for a totally indulgent soak. Add a few drops of essential oil to enhance the experience. Try lavender if you need calming or have a headache, rosemary if you are tired and sore, chamomile if you're ready for sleep, rose for an uplifting experience, or eucalyptus or peppermint to clear your head. Alternately, scatter rose petals in your bath water.

Or take it even a step further. The Japanese have a centuries-old tradition of bathing their feet in sake to soften and whiten them. Choose a moderately priced sake and mix it in a large bowl with some warm water for a therapeutic foot soak after a long hike or hard day on your feet—and don't forget to treat yourself to a glass on the side to soften the spirit.

Ask Cleopatra

Speaking of beverages for soaking, take a leaf out of Cleopatra's book and luxuriate in a bath with a quart of milk added to it, another very softening and soothing bath for silky skin.

A Hair Tonic from the Cupboard

Napa Valley stylist Bill Lefever suggests trying an occasional final rinse with white vinegar. It will balance the acid (pH) balance of your hair, tighten the follicles, and leave you with a glossier crowning glory.

Here are a few other recipes from Villagio's spa for pampering, luscious body treatments made from seasonal produce.

Pumpkin-Pineapple Pedicure

When pumpkins are at their peak, this treatment is offered at Villagio's spa—it's a great one for before that halloween party! The combination of pumpkin, pineapple, and honey is invigorating, hydrating, and exfoliating.

Cut a fresh, peeled pumpkin into small chunks, enough for about 2 to 3 cups. Place in a blender with 1/4 cup honey, 1 cup fresh pineapple chunks, 2 cloves, and a pinch of nutmeg. Blend to a smooth paste then apply a thick coat to feet and lower legs. Relax for 5 minutes then rinse off with warm water.

Honey Steam Body Wrap

This treatment has been used for hundreds of years for its conditioning, antibacterial, and healing properties.

Pour 1 to 2 cups of sea salt and 1 to 2 cups of honey in a microwavable bowl or a double boiler. Heat to just warm, being very careful not to overheat. Hot honey can burn your skin, so take care! Run a hot shower with the door closed to make your own steam room. Step into the shower and cleanse yourself with an aromatic body gel. Rinse off then step out of the shower and pat yourself dry. Apply the salt and honey mixture all over your body. Wrap yourself in a warm towel and leave on for 10 minutes while you sit and inhale the steam. Rinse off and apply your favorite lotion.

There are so many choices for different treatments at spas, it can almost be more stressful making a decision on what's going to be best for you than the stress you are hoping to relieve. Maybe you're going away for a spa holiday or perhaps you'd just like to try a treatment at a day spa down the road. Whatever the reason, it's good to know what some of the choices are and how to choose the best one for you, personally. Villagio's spa director offers tips to help you choose a treatment to bring you the most relaxation and pleasure or achieve the desired therapeutic effect.

MASSAGE

All massages have a common basis of bringing relief from stress and tension, encouraging deep breathing, and improved circulation, but the level of intensity is important to consider when making your choice. Massage also has an emotional component. The therapy of touch makes massage wonderful for those who are experiencing emotional stress, such as grieving or other difficult life situations. Massages are also a wonderful way of feeling pampered and glowing. Don't forget, drink lots of water after all massages to cleanse and rehydrate your system. Villagio offers cucumber water for its additional cleansing properties. To make your own, simply steep fresh slices of cucumber in a large jug of purified water.

Wellness or Swedish Massage

This is the most gentle of massages and is best for anyone who has never had or rarely has massages. The massage will improve circulation, while having a very relaxing and tension-relieving effect. It's a great choice for general stress relief, easing tired or stiff muscles, general aches and pains, or for helping you recover from jet lag.

Deep Tissue Massage (also called Sports Massage)

You may not want to choose this as your first massage or if it's been a long time since you've had a massage, as it can be quite intense. The pressure is much deeper, so it will have a greater effect on relieving sore muscles. However, if you have some specific areas of concern, such as shoulder soreness from sitting at a computer all day, you could combine a wellness massage with focused deep tissue work on just those areas. This is a great massage for athletes as it helps reduce muscle pain. It's also a great choice for those with tension aches and pains or muscle soreness. Regular deep tissue massage is wonderful for encouraging deep breathing and improving circulation, as well as helping to break down long-term tight muscles or knots. Just don't forget, drink lots of water directly after your massage as well as the following day.

Hot Stone Massage

Round, smooth, flat river stones are warmed to bath temperature and placed on accupressure points or tight spots on your body during the massage. The heated stones help bring blood to the surface to relieve tension points. It's an ideal choice for those that want something a little different and enjoy the warmth brought by the stones. The therapeutic effects are the same as the chosen massage.

FACIALS

Often neglected by men, these are great treatments for both sexes for cleansing, toning, removing dead skin cells, and hydrating the skin. The general process is a deep cleansing followed by a wash. Then, depending on your skin type, a mask is applied. It may be to balance and normalize if your skin is prone to oiliness, or hydrate if you tend to be dry. This is usually followed by an exfoliation to remove impurities, and to prepare your skin to receive the nutrients and moisture from the cream to follow. The final step is to apply a cream to nourish and hydrate your skin, which is specifically selected for your skin type.

Facials are wonderful for everyone, whether as a relaxing treatment to revive your skin and give you a glowing radiance before a dinner or special event, or just helping to restore the skin's suppleness and luster from exposure to harmful elements. If you work in a business that uses air conditioning, have had a long flight, are an avid athlete or swimmer, or your skin just feels like it needs a lift, try a facial—you'll feel like a new person, and a pampered one.

BODY TREATMENTS

There are many of these available and you should ask your spa for information on their specific programs. Here are two popular body treatments offered at Villagio Inn & Spa.

Grapeseed Body Polish

To first prepare your skin for the treatment, the skin is rubbed with a dry brush. This is followed by gentle massage with crushed grape seeds to promote exfoliation. A warm oil is then applied to hydrate, soothe, and nourish the smoothed skin. The grapeseed also contains vitamins A, C, and E. This is a great treatment to indulge in before a massage to allow your skin to soak up the richness of the massage oils. It will leave you feeling cleansed and radiant. It is often chosen by people at the end of a long winter to revive the body from months in heating and thick clothing. It's like a facial for your body!

Grapeseed Mud Wrap

Crushed grape seeds and clay are applied to the whole body to replace lost minerals and nourish the skin with vitamins A, C, and E from the seeds. It's a wonderful way to help your body and soul recover from a cold, illness, or course of antibiotics.

AQUATHERAPY

The idea of a bath—lounging in a warm aromatic pool of water—is the ultimate relaxation for anyone. Here is an example of a bath you might consider for a spa treatment.

Tuscan Deep Soak (or Japanese Deep Soak)

In this bath, you are immersed up to your neck in water that is kept between a very sedating 101–104 degrees. Aromatic oils of your choice are added depending on the therapeutic effect you desire (see the aromatherapy guide on page 137 for ideas on oils and scents). Sea salt is also added to the water to replenish minerals and then you luxuriate for 20 to 30 minutes. This is a wonderful treatment to calm your mind and spirit and allow you to slow down and decompress. You will find this bath helps remove the mental clutter of day-to-day stress and allows clearer thinking.

PEDICURE

The feet are so often neglected and yet are so vital to everyday living. They take us where we want to go, yet they get bound up in tight shoes and rarely moisturized, so we pay with calluses and other foot problems. The feet also contain pressure points that are wonderful to massage, as in the practice of reflexology. Taking time for a pedicure where your feet are immersed in warm water with therapeutic oils, such as refreshing peppermint, while they rest on smooth river stones is a wonderfully relaxing and therapeutic treatment for men and women alike. A pedicure will also soften callused areas and help relieve stressed calves. A pedicure is a great treatment if you're on your feet all day or have just put your feet through a demanding hike or run.

These are just a few of the many treatments offered at spas. If you have any medical conditions or back injury or strain, please consult with your doctor before undertaking any treatment. For more information on baths and aromatherapy, see pages 138 and 136.

Aromas can add a whole new dimension to your life. Just think of the many aromas in everyday living that can trigger warm, pleasant feelings and memories—fresh baking bread, the smell of rain after a long dry spell, a rose in full bloom, grapes at harvest, coffee brewing, fresh clean laundry—everyone has their own aroma experiences they associate with certain emotions.

There are also many aromas we can introduce into our lives that can create a mood, bring about a health benefit, or simply gratify our senses. Essential oils are the purest form of these aromas and the most common way of achieving their benefits. They can be used in a number of ways: burned or placed in vaporizers, diluted in a carrier oil, such as grapeseed or almond, as a massage oil, or dissolved in milk for the bath. Many people also like to add a few drops to a tissue to inhale throughout the day or on a compress to apply to muscular aches. You can also add a few drops to a bowl of hot water and cover your head with a towel to form your own personal inhalation chamber.

Because they are so highly concentrated, most essential oils should be not be used straight on the skin. They are also not advised for children, pregnant women, or those with specific medical conditions, so always consult with your doctor if you are unsure.

Following are some common aromatic oil suggestions and their applications to bring a taste of the aromatic spa to your home, and some tips on using them. There are many oils to choose from—these are just a few. Experiment with your own blends and find what works best for you personally as everyone has their own individual scent reactions.

STIMULATING SCENTS

Peppermint

Cooling and invigorating, uplifting for the senses and revitalizing for the skin. Try it in the bath or in massage oil, or add to a body cream to apply after a workout. Inhale the steam as a decongestant and to clear the head.

Lemon

Uplifting, refreshing, and stimulating for the senses. Increases mental alertness, so it's great as an office vaporizer scent.

Rosemary

Stimulating, invigorating, and great for fatigue. Add it to a bath after a long day of gardening or working to relieve muscles. Said to stimulate the senses and add luster to the hair, especially for brunettes.

Tangerine

Uplifting, stimulating, energizing, and refreshing in the bath.

Geranium

An astringent that stimulates the circulation. Refreshing and balancing for sensitive skin. Add it to massage oil or the bath to refresh the mind.

RELAXING SCENTS

Lavender

Calming, relaxing, and sleep inducing. Rub a couple of drops on your temples to relieve tension headaches, or place a few drops on your pillow or in your bedtime bath.

Chamomile

Soothes the mind and body, encourages sleep, and balances and tones the skin. Drink chamomile tea before bed and make extra to rinse your hair to bring out blond highlights. Keep the tea bags to place on the eyes to relieve computer strain. Add the oil to baths or night cream to balance the skin.

Bergamot

The scent of Earl Grey tea. Relaxing, uplifting, and deodorizing. This makes a wonderful room scent and morale booster. Enjoy a few drops in the bath before a big event.

HEAD-CLEARING SCENTS

Eucalyptus

Even though the leaves keep koala bears in a deep twenty-hour sleep, for humans the oil is invigorating, head clearing, and cleansing. Use as a steam inhalation for colds, or try a few drops in the bath to relieve muscular aches and pains. (The pure oil is also the best thing I've found for removing that sticky residue left on bottles from labels).

Pine

A fresh and clean aroma, great as a room deodorizer. Relieves cold symptoms when inhaled and stimulates circulation in massage oil or the bath.

ROMANTIC AND FEMININE SCENTS

Vanilla

Sweet, comforting, and alluring aroma making a wonderful bath oil or body oil before a night out.

Ylang-Ylang

Sweet and floral, calming and seductive, a great massage or bath oil. Let the scent circulate in the room to ease anxiety.

Rose

A deep, rich, and sensual aroma that is also calming. Great for sensitive skin. Add rosewater to your skin toner and a few drops of the oil to face cream for sensitive skin.

The ritual of bathing is one that has been enjoyed for centuries for purposes of both health and simple indulgence or relaxation. There are few ways to feel more luxurious before a dinner than to have a long relaxing and scented bath. Or slip straight from a bath to cool clean sheets for a long restful slumber. Creating the right environment will help to enhance your bath experience and bring you a greater sense of pleasure and well-being. Here are a few ideas:

* Light the bathroom dimly with candles or a soft lamp and turn on some smooth soft music.

* Apply a face mask before you immerse yourself and drench some cotton pads with rosewater to place over your eyes. Cucumber slices are also great to refresh your eyes, and, if you have eye-strain, apply cool damp chamomile tea bags to help reduce swelling and ease the tension.

* Make the bath as luxurious as possible—toss in some rose or geranium petals, bath salts or bubble bath, or some skin-softening milk. Oatmeal dissolved in the water is also very soothing.

* Choose an essential oil to bring you a sensual or therapeutic experience. Just emulsify a few drops in milk or rice milk. If you prefer not to use milk, put a few drops in the water after the tub is filled and swish around. Otherwise the oils will evaporate too quickly and leave you with a scentless bath. Try lavender, chamomile, or ylang-ylang to relax, destress, or induce sleep; peppermint or tangerine to invigorate or revive, eucalyptus to relieve sore muscles, and rosemary for fatigue. For more aroma ideas and their effects, turn to page 137.

* If you prefer, place the scents in a steam dispenser, or add a few drops to a warm damp face cloth, cover your face, and breathe deeply.

* Pour yourself a glass of champagne or just sip a cup of tea. The tea will stimulate perspiration that will refresh you further.

* To avoid that wrinkly skin look, keep your bath to less than 20 minutes, and if you are using oils don't have the water too hot or they will evaporate.

* If you're game, try ending your bath with a cool shower—it is very refreshing and the Swiss say it helps strengthen your immune system.

Mood Colors—
For Relaxation, Stimulation, and Well-Being

Color can have a very profound effect on everyday life. The colors we choose to surround ourselves with can greatly influence the mood we create, whether through furnishings or wall colors for the home or office, clothes, or even our computer screens.

Aside from the psychological and physical responses that are associated with different colors, there is an individual personal element as well. Many colors can cause us to react in certain ways because of similar colors in nature that bring us pleasure, reflection, comfort, or excitement. We also might associate different colors with experiences and memories. For example, your grandmother may have had a wonderful crimson bedspread that you loved to climb on and snuggle in, so this color may bring out a sense of warmth and nurturing for you. If you love the ocean, sea blue may give you a sense of peace and relaxation, or if you are stirred by a deep, rich sunset, these tones in a room may energize and stimulate you. You have to explore for yourself to build your own pleasing world of color.

Following you will find some ideas for using color to create the mood you desire, including some insight from Villagio's architect, Bruce Pao of IPA Design in Berkeley, California, and interior designer, Charles DeLisle of Your Space.

Green: Serenity, tranquility, harmony, and balance are emotions often associated with greens, especially hues such as sage and forest greens, pastel greens, and the green of a freshly mowed lawn. Think of the bright appeal of a Granny Smith apple. Greens can lighten a mood; as the philosopher Pliny once said, "Emerald delights the eye without fatiguing it."

Touches of green on white are ideal for a hot room, such as a sunroom, to bring a sense of cool freshness. Green is also a wonderful color to choose for a room where restfulness and tranquility are the motives, especially if it is a room overlooking a garden and trees.

By repeating the colors you see outside, it will link the two harmoniously and bring the outdoors inside. Green has also been described as a color that gives many people a sense of healing and calm.

Teal, on the other hand, is sophisticated and can add an upscale look, so if you want to clothe yourself to boost confidence and feel that way, choose a teal scarf, tie, or dress.

Blue: Blues can bring a number of moods to a room, depending on the hue. Being a cool color, blues can be calming, harmonious, and relaxing. Think of the blue of a freshwater lake or a pale blue sky. Pastel blues can also bring a delicate or ethereal feeling. Deeper blues are more sophisticated, elegant, classy, and formal, even bringing a sense of subdued dignity, such as you might feel from a blue with purple tones. Deep blue is also great for libraries and can kindle a meditative mood.

The blue greens of the sea, such as aqua, bring a tranquil sense of space and coolness, while turquoise is more lively and even gives a sense of glistening. If you're after a radiant look, this could be your color.

If you want your bathroom to look like a spa, try a sage blue green. Blue and green in harmony are said to create a tranquil aura to relax, refresh, and replenish.

Blue with black is the look to choose for an authoritative or serious air, and brilliant blue adds energy and electricity to the air.

Purple: Combining the peace and comfort of blue with the energy and fire of red will give you the enigmatic color of purple. Purple is the color that has many faces and you find people often either love it or dislike it. It has so many different tones and can create a sense of passion and mystery or of quiet sophistication. It makes sense that the more red in purple, the more arousing it will be. The more blue, the more serene. Picture the shades of grape, mulberry, and plum as décor in your living space. They will add a dignified, classic look. Mauve, lavender, and lilac will be more romantic and soothing, and even give a fragrant feel to a room, so these are great bathroom accessory colors. Purple can be ethereal, sensuous, regal, decadent, or magical, as it has so many different shades. You may not like the sense created by solid blocks of purple, but accents, like a huge bunch of lavender, may add just that touch needed for a splash of life, romance, or intrigue.

Red: Red is boldness and excitement, energy and passion, seduction and temptation. In its purest form in clothing, whether a red dress or a red tie or handkerchief, it can give a look of sensuality or confidence, and can be very empowering. It says, "Stop and look." In your environment, it can invigorate and stimulate, add vibrancy and depth. It can be a color that stirs emotions, helps overcome tiredness, and quickens the pulse.

In its more subdued forms, such as ruby, crimson, and claret, a rich dignity can be achieved. Think of a dining room with chairs of claret velvet—there's enough energy to stimulate appetite and conversation, yet its rich elegance can formalize a room. Or try a deep toasty rust red lounge in a "hideaway" room to escape to with a book and a glass of wine. Pale rose–colored walls bring soft romance to the bedroom, especially when accented with the seductive splash of a ruby pillow on a white bed.

Pink, on the other hand, with pure, cool, clean white offsetting the energy of red, is soft, feminine, nurturing, and comforting. In bolder forms it can be uplifting and lessen the "sweet as candy" look. It is cozy and romantic and can be stress relieving.

When thinking of the effect that red shades have on you, imagine your response to sunsets. Some are a deep red with blue clouds, almost as if the sky is on fire. Others are a pale pink hue that lights the sky and shines out from behind the clouds. Is one more "stirring" than the other, one more peaceful and calming?

The **orange** side of red brings in happy yellow and can be fun and outgoing, appetite and conversation stimulating, and revitalizing. For a more elegant and soothing presence, opt for the softer tones of peach and cantaloupe.

Yellow: The bright, happy, sunny, and warm color of the sun and sand, or the inside of a glowing fire, yellow is visually livening and playful. It makes great kitchen color (unless you don't want to have your appetite stimulated)! Yellow splashes in a room can bring in the sunshine, add warmth and coziness, or lift the mood in a dark room. It is also said to make a room appear larger and stimulate thought, but may inhibit sleep, so don't go overboard in the bedroom or your nightwear.

Mustard and ochre are more restful on the eyes and can bring an earthy, meditative feel to a room. These deeper hues of yellow can also level down the tone of a room to give a feeling of comfort and contemplation, but stimulate thinking and meditation. Mustard is a great color for a feature office wall, or try a brighter mustard if more active than passive thinking is required.

These are just a few of the vast color palettes at our fingertips and some common associations. Everyone is an individual, however, and you will need to experiment to build your own world of color.

Healthy Business—Exercise, Eating Right, and Mental Clarity When Traveling on Business

Earning an income consumes the vast majority of most adults' waking hours. Often times as well, the hours required or the conditions of our jobs aren't the most conducive to our health, especially if you're tied for long hours to a desk and computer or have to travel constantly.

There are numerous ways to make your place of work and business travel better for your general health, leaving you with more energy and less tension, and probably just a little happier about leaving home each morning.

AT THE OFFICE

* If you are deskbound most of the day, create a positive environment around you with elements of life that bring a smile to your face. Bring flowers, a plant, family photos, or an aroma dispenser for your desk. If you are able to, paint your walls in an inspiring color, or just paint a feature wall—try yellow, orange, or mustard or see page 140 on colors for more ideas.

* Drink lots of water. Air conditioning is very drying to your skin and dehydrating as well. Always have a bottle of water on hand or try a glass of water with lime or lemon slices to uplift and refresh you. Bring a spray bottle of water with a few drops of your favorite aromatic oil to spray on your face—try lavender, rose, or peppermint. Lavender will also help relieve tension headaches.

* Have healthy snacks on hand, especially if it's a day when you don't think lunch is going to happen. Regular healthy snacks help to keep you energized and free from cravings. Try nuts, seeds, and dried fruit, rice cakes or crackers, fresh fruit or vegetables, yogurt, whole-grain bread or bagels, or make a smoothie (see page 125).

* Remember to keep moving. Get up from your desk at regular intervals, even if just to walk around the desk itself. At lunchtime, walk instead of driving to the local café. Take the stairs rather than the elevator and, if you catch the bus to work, get off a stop

or two earlier, and walk the rest of the way. It may help to inspire you if you keep a pair of comfy walking shoes at work.

* Keep those hands, legs, and shoulders from cramping. Rotate your wrists and ankles regularly, give your colleague a shoulder massage, and always remember to stretch. Massage your hands all over if they are getting sore, paying special attention to tender points.

* Don't forget to breathe. The brain needs oxygen to function properly and we often tend to breathe very shallowly, especially when tired or stressed. Keep something on your desk to remind you to take time to breathe deeply, right down to your stomach—even if it's just a sticky note on your computer saying, "breathe."

* Step away and revive yourself if you get too overwhelmed by decisions and chores. Take a quick walk outside to declutter your head and think more clearly.

* Take your shoes off and allow your feet to breathe and be free of the constriction of shoes. Keep some smooth round stones on the floor to rub your feet over to massage your pressure points.

* Above all, don't let the little things pull you down or stress you— write them on a piece of paper and throw them in the trash as a sign of your rebellion!

STEVE ZANETELL, EXERCISE PHYSIOLOGIST AT
YOUNTVILLE FITNESS AND HEALTH CLUB, OFFERS
SOME IDEAS FOR STRETCHING AND MOVING AT WORK

* Every hour sit up straight, tuck your chin in, pull your shoulders back and raise your hands up over your back as though lifting weights. This is great for stretching your back and shoulders. Leaning forward in your seat and touching the floor will stretch your lower back.

* If you are on your feet all day, put one foot up on a low stool, then alternate with the other, to help relieve lower back tension. Stretch your leg on a chair and keep your body moving and constantly shifting. Similarly, those who are sitting all day may benefit by occasionally using a exercise ball, which keeps you constantly shifting to balance and helps to stabilize your posture and muscles. You can buy these at many sporting goods stores.

* If your job requires repetitive movement, do standing stretches that reverse the action you are doing.

HEALTHY TRAVEL

Frequent travel and healthy living often seem like a contradiction in terms. Most of us have good intentions, but flight delays, dinner offers, hectic schedules, and cocktails often win out over workouts and other healthy intentions. If it's only every now and then you may not mind. But even so, if you just do a little planning ahead to make your trip a healthier one, you'll be rewarded by having more energy and focus, and come home revived rather than exhausted.

* Flying is very dehydrating. Make sure you drink lots of water and limit the amount of coffee and alcohol you enjoy. Try a nice moisturizing mask after the flight.

* Choose the right hotel. Do some research to find a hotel with a good gym, pool, or place to run. It's a great way to prepare for the day or unwind after a long day.

* Does it have a good breakfast buffet? Starting the day with a substantial healthy breakfast will give you energy until lunch.

* Walk to dinner. Choose a hotel in walking distance of good restaurants. You'll get more exercise, sleep better, and save the cost of a cab.

* Make lighter dinner choices. Large heavy meals can weigh you down and leave you drained and sluggish the next day. Try ordering two appetizers or a salad and appetizer or select dishes with more vegetable components than meat and rich sauces.

* Chase wine with water. Make a point of drinking as much water as you do wine—you'll reap the rewards the next day.

If you are organizing a conference, build in a few healthy elements:

* Have cucumber water with lime on hand all day for conferees— it's cleansing, refreshing, and invigorating. Simply steep fresh slices of cucumber and lime in a large jug of purified water.

* Serve healthy choices for snacks and lunch.

* Treat conferees to a massage or spa treatment to make them feel revived and important.

* Build an exercise component into the program, whether it's tennis, a town walk, a hike, or game of golf.

* Don't forget a relaxing social component. If you are treating your conferees to a nice hotel with great facilities, make sure they have time to enjoy them.

Everyone has his or her own prescription for health, and we are all different. Find the one that's right for you, regardless of what your friends and colleagues or magazines say. You are the one who needs to enjoy your life and there's no point taking on anything you don't enjoy—it will never last.

Quick Pick=Me=Ups
(and Other Remedies to Live By)

Do you find yourself lacking energy just to perform normal day-to-day activities? Are you caught in a catch-22 of wanting to exercise to boost your stamina but don't have the stamina to get going? There are some simple steps you can take to boost your energy level, but keep in mind that if there seems to be no reason for your lethargy, you may want to schedule a checkup with your doctor.

Enjoy a nourishing breakfast of foods that will last the distance. Try whole grain bread, muesli or high fiber cereal, fruit, or even a smoothie (try some of the blends on page 125). You'll find that a good breakfast will eliminate midmorning slumps and cravings for coffee and sweets.

Keep up the fluids. Don't wait until you are thirsty to drink water. If you're feeling sluggish or run-down, you may actually be dehydrated, especially if you're an active person Try to drink at least six to eight glasses of water a day. It's okay for some of this liquid to be in the form of juice, herbal tea, and so forth, but pure, refreshing water is the best.

Eat foods that have staying power. Many foods, such as sugar, will give you a zap of instant energy but leave you "zapped" shortly after. Other foods will give you a gradually released supply of energy that will last longer. Good foods to consider are pasta, grains such as oats and whole-grain breads and bagels, long grain rice, beans and lentils, new potatoes and yogurt. If you eat these with foods such as nuts, milk, and lean protein foods, that will make their energy-giving power last even longer.

Don't go overboard on alcohol, tea, and coffee. A little can be therapy, a lot is not.

Make sure you are eating all your energy nutrients. Iron, vitamin C and the B group, magnesium, potassium, and calcium are some of the nutrients that help in the energy-producing process. Eating a balanced diet rich in fruits, vegetables, grains, fish, lean meat, and dairy will help ensure you are getting your daily supply of essential nutrients. You may want to buy yourself a handbook or quick reference guide to the foods rich in these nutrients.

Forget the diet. Instead of depriving your body of the food it needs to function properly, and the pleasure of eating, tip the energy balance the other way and burn calories with exercise. Dieting will actually slow your metabolic rate, but exercise has the opposite effect, even if it's just brisk walking.

Sleep. There's nothing that will make you feel less like moving than plain old tiredness. Try to get at least six to eight hours of sleep each night.

Getting Physical—You've Got to Move!

We all want to be healthy—fit and trim, with lots of energy—and to look and feel good. Yet many of us rely solely on what we eat, or resort to wonder supplements and strict diets in our quest to accomplish this goal. What we so often forget is that one of the most important ways to get healthy and stay healthy, and also to help prevent a range of chronic illnesses, is simply to *move* more.

This doesn't have to mean breaking your budget to buy all the latest gear, running ten miles, or really doing anything you don't want to. It just means finding an activity or two that you enjoy and getting physical every day. Exercise can be a great energy booster, too; even if you're tired after a long, hard day, a short walk or bike ride may be the best thing for you.

Before you begin any exercise program, there are a few steps to take:

* If you have any health problems, check with your doctor to make sure the activity is appropriate for you.

* Don't forget to breathe. Deep breathing allows more oxygen to get to your muscles for energy and also tends to improve your posture by making you stand tall.

* Start out slower and gradually increase the intensity and duration over the days and weeks.

* Take time to recuperate if you don't feel well or if you have aches and pains.

* Enjoy a variety of activities to bring your whole body the most benefit and stick to activities that are comfortable and pleasurable for you—if you don't want to smile (inside or out) while you're doing it, try something else.

* Before you get moving, try to find time to warm up and stretch the major muscle groups that you'll be using. Then allow yourself a slow cooldown of at least five minutes and another stretch afterward rather than just stopping and jumping into the shower.

Now that you're ready, motivated, and armed, Steve Zanetell, MA, PTA, exercise physiologist, trainer, and owner of Yountville Fitness and Health Club, offers some tips for getting more action into your life for a healthier, happier you. He also has advice for keeping our bodies in the best condition we can for the demands of everyday living, no matter what your age, shape, and sex, along with ways to build strength, flexibility, and endurance. Remember, as you age, conditioning and stretching become even more important to help you avoid injuries.

* Enjoy a walk. Walking is one of the best, safest, and most enjoyable ways to stay in shape. Just twenty minutes or more of brisk walking can do wonders, not only to help keep you trim and build your cardiovascular health, but also to destress, unwind, and be social—for many it's also a great health benefit for your dog! Try a quick morning pace to get the blood flowing and plan your day, or a social walk with colleagues at lunch. There are few things better for getting a good night's sleep than an after-dinner walk. Plan weekend outings that will involve some walking, a trail hike, or just seeing the sights.

* Go for a bicycle ride or roller-blading—think of them as alternatives to the car for getting to the shops.

* Try a yoga or tai chi class to help reduce stress, increase flexibility, and loosen up. It's amazing how much stress we hold in our muscles that a weekly yoga or stretching class can help alleviate. Another great way to increase flexibility is to do the "Superman" stretch. Lay flat on your tummy and raise your arms and legs and stretch like Superman soaring through the sky.

* Build strength and confidence with weight or resistance training. Take your arms, for example, and think of how much we rely on them to carry and lift things, and yet we often forget that we need to condition them. This is especially important as we age because we lose muscle mass. Swimming is a great arm strengthener as are push-ups. A good exercise for building back and leg strength is to sit against a wall as though there is a chair under you and hold for a minute (or as long as you can). Many people use this exercise to strengthen their legs before ski season.

* Pick a sport you enjoy and get involved on weekends or in other free time you may have. Tennis, volleyball, racquetball, indoor soccer, karate, kickboxing—all are great for building health and comradeship.

Learn to Relax

Laughter is wonderful medicine for the spirit. Do it whenever you can.

Within the busy lives many of us lead these days, it's easy to forget to take time out to stop and unwind. It often seems as though the wonders of modern technology, including cell phones and email, have left us in a continual state of being on call. And then we become so used to being busy that we feel guilty if we stop, and so deny ourselves that crucial relaxation or personal time. It's no wonder that we suddenly find ourselves less productive at what we do and constantly tired or distracted. Most of us also have certain barriers that prevent us from getting the relaxation we need. So explore your own life and find where you can squeeze in some time-out. Take time to relax. You and those around you will reap the benefits. Here are some ideas.

Do you jump up from the dinner table and get straight into the housework or back to the computer? Try just clearing the dishes then sitting and snuggling with your family in front of the television for a while. Or maybe play a board game. The housework can wait.

Do you grab a sandwich and sit at the computer over lunch? Try taking a walk or going to a local café and reading a magazine instead. You'll probably find that the time out will make the rest of your day more productive and efficient.

Are meals for you a hurricane around the kitchen, and a mad gobble down? Try going out for a bite and enjoying relaxed conversation around the table, without dishes to clean.

Do you cram weekends with cleaning and garden work and find that if you stay at home, there's always something to be done? Make a point of getting out for at least an hour or, better still, a whole day, whether for a hike, bike ride, picnic, or just plain fun shopping—whatever brings you and those with you the most pleasure.

How often do you just stop and look? Next time you find yourself just sitting and looking at something—a flower, the ocean, birds playing, or rain falling—and suddenly feel like you've just wasted time, stay and look some more. It's very therapeutic.

Is music your passion? Even if not, just sitting with your eyes closed and listening to music can be very relaxing. Allow your mind to drift with the tune. Or learn a musical instrument. Sitting and playing the piano, drumming, or playing the guitar or any musical instrument allows you to stop, relax, and unwind, and the artistry can be very rewarding for the soul, too.

Learn a meditative technique and try to practice it daily. There are a number of different ways of meditating practiced around the world, and you don't have to travel to the Far East to learn one. Meditation is simply allowing yourself to focus and balance through relaxation. Most important, it's time that you devote to yourself.

If you need a distraction to get you to slow down, try a massage or take a creative class in something—cooking, art, pottery. Or do something on your own that you keep saying you must—visit a gallery, go wine tasting, or go to a movie.

Don't allow the months to pass without taking a break and getting away. Even if we love what we do, we all need time to get away for a vacation from the work environment and give ourselves some pampering and relaxation time.

Take time out for a luxurious foot bath while you read the paper. Try one of the recipes on page 130.

Sleep. Everyone needs a good night's sleep, and taking time out to relax will help, but there are other ways people have found to help them to sleep peacefully and soundly each night. Don't eat a heavy meal late at night, or, if you do, go for a walk afterward. Try a cup of chamomile tea or warm milk before retiring and avoid highly caffeinated drinks in the evening. Try a lavender pillow, lavender oil rubbed on your temples, or a bedtime lavender-scented bath, and remember to breathe deeply.

Afterword

I hope that this book will enrich your life with good food, relaxation ideas, and a spirit of well-being. And most of all, may it inspire you to experience your own escape to Yountville.

Index

terrine, heirloom tomato and egg-plant, 42–44
tomatillo-avocado sauce, salmon tacos with pasilla chile aioli and, 80
tomato(es)
    blanching and peeling, 44, 75
    "marmelade", sautéed fillet of John Dory with heirloom toma-to vinaigrette and, 74–75
    See also cherry tomato; heirloom tomato
Torralba, Eric, 64–65, 86
trout
    river, potato-crusted, 72
    smoked, and salmon rillette, 7
truffle(s)
    Périgord, with fricassee of sum-mer sweet onions and truffle glace, 26–27
    truffle mashed potatoes, slow-roasted salmon with wilted spinach and, 66
tuna
    ahi, nori-wrapped tempura, sushi salad with, 58–59
    ahi sashimi, nori-crusted, with hijiki seaweed salad, 10
    albacore, grilled, salad, 83
turkey
    in Blues burger, 99
    wrapped in a farci crust, 96

vegetable(s)
    fricassee of summer sweet onions with Périgord truffles and truf-fle glace, 26–27

mixed spring, with fava bean-fresh herb sauce, 45
    stock, 22
    See also specific vegetable
venison, grilled, with Teleme cheese risotto and blackberry sauce, 95
Villagio Inn & Spa, 42–44, 55, 72
vinaigrettes, 10
    heirloom tomato, 74–75
    onion, 26–27
    raspberry, 36
    red wine, 29
    walnut, 36
vinegar, as hair tonic, 131

wake-up call, 125
walnut
    chocolate, date, and walnut meringue cake, 105
    sauce, linguini with broccoli, olives and, 50
    vinaigrette, for watermelon salad with prosciutto, arugula, and red onions, 36
warm roasted mushroom and feta salad, 34
watercress
    pasta with Zinfandel prawns, watercress, and mint-tarragon oil, 53
    shaved summer squash, water-cress, and chicken salad with blue cheese, 39
watermelon salad with prosciutto, arugula and red onions, 36
white bean minestrone with garlic and parmesan bruschetta, 20

wild rice and farro salad, 61
Wilmoth, Jude, 39, 95
wine
    as body soak, 130
    and cheese pairings, 118–19
    Moscato-mascarpone and berry mille-feuille, 111
    pairings, about, xvi
    pear, merlot, and olive oil cake, 108–9
    pinot noir, mussels steamed in, 77
    red wine and balsamic beef with pumpkin purée, 87
    red wine and pepper crackers with pear-white wine pâté, 9
    white wine, clams and prosciutto crumble, angel hair pasta with, 51
    Zinfandel prawns, pasta with watercress, mint-tarragon oil and, 53
winter squash and basil risotto with parmesan-macadamia shards, 56
wraps, Parma prosciutto, with balsamic dipping oil, 4

Yount, George Calvert, xv
Yountville Fitness and Health Club, 145
Yountville, history and events, xv–xvi

Zanetell, Steve, 145–46